KISSING OR NO KISSING

WHOM WILL YOU SAVE YOUR KISSES FOR?

A Dating Guide To Creating Your Dreams

To Steve, Jadwiga, Thomas & Emily,

January 2006

Here's to make a better world for both men & women.

KISSING OR NO KISSING
WHOM WILL YOU SAVE YOUR KISSES FOR?

A Dating Guide To Creating Your Dreams

Fléchelle Morin

First Edition

Cheval Publishing, Inc., Pacific Palisades, California

KISSING OR NO KISSING

WHOM WILL YOU SAVE YOUR KISSES FOR?

A Dating Guide To Creating Your Dreams

by Fléchelle Morin

Published by:
Cheval Publishing, Inc
Post Office Box 664
Pacific Palisades, CA 90272-0664 U.S.A.
Orders@ChevalPublishing.com
http://www.chevalpublishing.com

Library of Congress Cataloging-in-Publication Data

Morin, Flechelle.
    Kissing or no kissing : whom will you save your
    kisses for? : a dating guide to creating your dreams
    / by Flechelle Morin.
        p. cm.
    LCCN 2005903283
    ISBN 0-9766516-8-8

    1. Mate selection. 2. Dating (Social customs)
    3. Man-woman relationships.   I. Title.

HQ801.M67 2005   646.7'7
                          QBI05-600051

CONTENTS

Disclaimer

This book is designed to provide information on dating, negotiating, and relating with other human beings. It is sold with the understanding that the publisher and author are not engaged in rendering accounting, legal, medical, psychological and psychiatric advice, counseling or services, and/or other professional services. Psychological services of any nature should be sought directly from a licensed professional. The author is not a licensed therapist or medical professional.

The purpose of this book is to provide information and entertain. We cannot, and are not, assuming the role of your physician or therapist. The information provided in this book is not designed to replace the relationship that exists between a patient and his/her existing physician and therapist. The author and Cheval Publishing, Inc. shall have neither liability nor responsibility to any person or entity with respect to any loss or damage caused, or alleged to have caused, directly or indirectly, by the information contained in this book.

If you do not wish to be bound by the above, you may return this book, unread, to the publisher for a full refund.

All names and situations used as examples in this book have been changed to protect the innocent. Any resemblance to anybody you know, or to you or your situation, is only coincidental.

All quotations remain the intellectual property of their respective originators. Cheval Publishing, Inc. and Fléchelle Morin do not assert any claim of copyright for individual quotations other than the ones written by the author. All use of quotations is done under the fair use copyright principal.

. . .

Foreword

WE LIVE IN A VERY FAST-PACED WORLD. WE ARE MADE to believe that we want and need everything now. We are constantly bombarded by advertising and peer pressure, our community, our friends, and in some instances, our own families to conform to this hasty way of life, which we have come to believe is the right way to live. It is a life where instant gratification is not only accepted but also expected.

In her book *Kissing Or No Kissing ~ Whom Will You Save Your Kisses For?,* Fléchelle conveys in a very engaging way why taking a new look at a more traditional way of dating and relating with men is for women the antidote to dead end and ultimately heartbreaking relationships.

In my practice, I see many women who are beautiful, talented, successful and accomplished in their lives and careers. These very capable women, like so many of their generation who seem to have it all, yearn for families of their own. They have the willingness and the capacity for great love for a husband and children. They have much to offer, and yet, they are still single. They were told that they could have it all and that they were equal to the men they investigated relationships with. Many women found that the battle to achieve equality with men was stiff and challenging, to say the least. At the soul level, these women want love, affection, caring, protection, and—most of all—to belong. They want to come home to families who love them, need them, and rely on them.

Fléchelle's sentient sensitivity allows her to sympathize with these women's desires and be supportive of their wants and needs. She recognizes the challenge they are faced with as they approach such a crucial point in their lives as choosing a mate for themselves, and she helps them make the necessary behavioral changes which allow them to put sincere tangible efforts into their quests to find husbands for themselves and fathers for their children.

I have dedicated a large part of my life to helping people create more love and understanding through practicing cognizant communication skills with the human beings they come across in their life paths. Fléchelle has managed to write a book that does just that: give the opportunity for women to capture loving, caring and responsible interpersonal life skills. I can only hope this book will reach many, as there is no telling of the changes that could occur all around us if people start to consciously love one another and appropriately communicate with each other.

In order to reach their goals, women will most certainly benefit from reading this book as they will find within its pages the necessary tools to achieve their dreams of being married and creating the families they want.

Pat Allen, Ph.D.

Dr. Pat Allen is the author of *Conversational Rape*, co-author of *Getting To "I Do"* and *Staying Married And Loving It,* and is the creator of the *WANT*® *technique of semantic realignment.*

Introduction

*Many of the insights of the saints stem
from their experience as sinners.*

Eric Hoffer

IF YOU ARE STILL SINGLE WITH LITTLE PROSPECT OF MARRYING in the next year, and you are really serious about getting married, then this book is for you. If you have the guts and the dedication to make your dreams come true but only need a road map to reach and stay on the path to have a successful relationship leading to marriage, then again, this book is for you.

There are good books such as the innovative and thought provoking *Getting To "I Do"* by Dr. Pat Allen and Sandra Harmon that will guide you through the process of recognizing yourself and finding your place in your relationship of choice and the brilliant *He's Just Not That Into You: The No-Excuse Truth To Understanding Guys* by Greg Behrendt and Liz Tuccillo that will help you recognize that you are hanging onto the wrong guy and how to stop wasting your time on unworthy men.

Kissing Or No Kissing ~ Whom Will You Save Your Kisses For? will not only tell you why you were uncontrollably bonded to some men you've been wasting your time with, it will tell you how not to get bonded to a man before you get the commitment you want from him first. *Kissing Or No Kissing ~ Whom Will You Save Your Kisses For?* will help you relate in healthy ways with the men you will choose to date. Also you will learn how to migrate from toxic men to healthy men.

This book is not for the faint at heart. This book is especially written to help women get on the path to marriage. If you do not want to marry and simply want to have a boyfriend or even just have casual relationships, this book and even parts of this way of dating will also help you in the process of selecting a better partner for your relationship of choice, as you will learn how to recognize your wants and needs and negotiate a better deal for you both. If you are gay or lesbian and want to be in a relationship where you would be the feminine energy complementary partner to a masculine energy man or woman, you will also gain from reading this book. This book is about having loving relationships with other human beings. With any luck, it could even help you have better relationships with all the men and masculine energy women in your life. It would bring me great happiness to know that this book might have helped you in having better relationships with your sons, grandfathers, father, stepfather, father-in-law, uncles, brothers, nephews, male co-workers, the entire male community, along with the masculine energy women you already know and the ones you will come in contact with.

Primarily, this program is designed to help women achieve their goal of marrying into a covenant relationship and creating their very own families. This lifestyle can be yours if you are ready to follow this simple plan.

I know that many of you will tell me that this program seems so backward, that in fact, it defies the evolution of our society and demerits how hard we have fought to bring equality between men and women. Well, I must tell you that I do not believe that the feminist movement has been to the benefit of men, women and children when it comes to personal real life application and happiness. There are more and more lonely and isolated men and women. Of course, because of the equality movement, we have indeed much more than our parents materially, but this system has failed to prove to me that men and women are happier when it comes to their personal lives.

Your first impression of the book might be that this is a challenging dating program and that you are way above what is written here; however, I believe that you might find a point or two that may interest you. You might be shocked out of your socks, or you might simply just hate what you read here and simply think that this is just too ridiculous to be tried. For all of you I say: "Put aside the book and keep dating the way you've been doing. In a year or two, when you are still single, pick up this book again, and give it another try. By then, you might be ready to re-evaluate your way of thinking about men and dating."

Although this program will seem very difficult in the beginning, with some simple behavioral modifications you will find that this program is not only easy, but the new you won't want to revert to the way you used to date, as you will look at men and masculinity in a much more positive light. You will find that negotiating better agreements between you and the men you will date will empower you and help you stay centered within your femininity.

Another thing: if you like bad boys, this book won't help you much. This book is to help women get in contact with good men. If you like the exciting type, this book will not help you much either, as it has been written to help women find and get engaged to family type men whose excitement is to come home at the end of their work days and spend time with their wives and children. So if you are addicted to the exciting type that will keep you on your toes by cheating on you, stealing from you, and continuously dishonoring you, this book won't do you any good since this dating philosophy has been designed to eliminate these "bad boys" out of a woman's life.

This program will keep you from falling into the arms of predators in disguise. Many unscrupulous men have no qualms about selling romance to gullible women. Armed with this new knowledge, you will learn how to minimize the risk of finding yourself in compromising relationships and feel safer opening your heart to good men.

If you decide to put this program into practice today or in a decade from now, it will work for you. Follow these simple steps, and you will be on your way to being married.

INTRODUCTION

WHY ARE YOU STILL SINGLE?

Have you ever wondered why some women are married to great
guys, and their days seem to be filled with strolling their babies
in the park in the morning, lunching with girlfriends, afternoon
naps, and evenings out with their husbands and friends? They live
in nice homes and have plenty of help to make their lives easier
and more beautiful. Have you ever wondered why these men
never gave a second look at you and ended up marrying others?
Or perhaps you did not give a second look at such men... Well, if
you are brave enough to stick around and read this book and put
this program in practice, the question of why will be something
from the past.

It is no big secret that masculine men like to be in charge. Are
you a woman who is self-sufficient, independent, and does not
need a man in her life? If you answered yes to this question, then
you have the answer to the first reason why you are still single
and not married to the type of man who likes to take care of a
woman and children. Masculine men like to be needed, as they
are generous providers and relentless protectors. Masculine men
like to know that they can depend on their women as their women
can depend on them; they like interdependent women. You can
be an autonomous woman who likes to depend on her man and
allow him to take care of her; this creates the balance needed in
order for the yin and yang energy to flow freely in relationships
between masculine men and feminine women.

Although this book was written especially for women who
have chosen to be the yin feminine energy in their relationships—
and I will refer more to the relations between a yin energy female
and a yang energy male—if you choose to be the yang energy
female in your relationship, this book will also be helpful to you
by first making you aware of your true spirited nature and how to
honor yourself and make healthier choices for you and for your
feminine energy partner.

In this book, I will go into details about aspects of dating such
as verbal, physical, and emotional ways to relate to the various

men you will date, along with safety tips to follow while dating, including dating on the Internet. I will guide you on ways to relate with the opposite sex during your quest to find your future husband. You will learn how to value yourself, make and keep commitments for yourself, and communicate honestly your needs and wants with confidence in a precise and concise manner. The communication techniques you will learn from reading this book will not only help you to marry, but if applied in your daily life, will get you better relationships with your family and your friends and will get you more satisfying interactions in all your personal and professional relationships.

Why I wrote this book

I made the decision to write this book because I wanted to provide women with the necessary tools that would allow them to take the risk to go out there, date more than ever, and—most especially—date more wisely. I wanted to help women find a mate and experience all the beauty marriage can bring to the souls of two loving human beings.

I have a strong love for womankind and see the goodness inside women and their desire to receive love, give love, and create love. I love weddings with all the preparedness: wedding dress fittings, bridal showers, and all the fun and positive nervousness such an event brings to the bride, groom, their families and friends. I also love births. I love the smell of babies (after a bath), the softness of their skin and the promises which lie inside all new little human beings.

This book was written to help women find men with whom they could investigate future married lives together. The intent of this book is to have women take the risk to go out there in the dating world, empower them in their femininity, and help and encourage them to create attainable dreams—dreams which are most often already there, just waiting to be given the chance to have lives of their own.

This book covers the period from dating to engagement. Dating is what you do in order to find a potential suitor with whom you would be able to investigate a future married life, by committing to each other through the act of engagement, which if everything goes well, will take you to the action of marrying. The period from engagement to marriage is the subject of my next book.

I could not help myself writing this book, as it was more of a calling than anything else. In fact, it was one of the hardest things I have ever done. Frankly, I find it much easier to grow my own vegetables. Besides, it always gives me a great sense of accomplishment when I look at the jars containing the "Green Tomato Ketchup" I've made with the tomatoes I grew myself.

So why did I put myself on the line and at risk of the disapproval of some forever criticizing souls? Because the happiness I can bring into many women's lives by far surpasses the unpleasantness of the few critics.

I am grateful to have had the opportunity and the will to write this book.

I also want to add that I love men very much. I find life so much more interesting with men around. I have as much fun having a conversation with my mechanic as I have talking with a country leader.

I have been married and have memorable recollections of my life as a married woman. I also have unforgettable memories from my dating experience and of all the men who were generous enough to take me out and show me wonderful times, having fun and laughing until tears would come down our faces. I consider myself very lucky to have experienced that much enjoyment and to have had the chance to meet so many noble men.

I have also dated not so noble men. I dated men who lied about their marital status by telling me they were divorced, when, in fact, they were still married and living with their wives. I have had men put drugs in my drink a couple of times. Although nothing bad happened to me as I was able to realize what they did before I was too intoxicated, it was nevertheless very scary. I even had a relationship with a man who turned out to give me little more than heartaches and headaches; this relationship ended on a bad note with the intervention of the law.

The mission of this book is to take you from being "single and unattached" to "single and attached" by being engaged, along with strong hopes and promises of getting married at the end of your courting venture.

I wish you the courage and the luck necessary for you to achieve as much.

How "Kissing Or No Kissing ~ Whom Will You Save Your Kisses For?" came to be

I think that we all can use some help when it comes to love matters. Some people seem to have a natural flair for it, but I think that most people have more questions than answers when it comes to dating and finding the right mate for them.

With this book, I want to bring at large the knowledge I gained while out there in the trenches of the dating world.

Dating has changed a great deal in the last few decades. One would think that being more permissive while dating would make everybody happier, right? Men would get what they want the most, sex, and women would get rewarded for being so generous with men, which in turn would make men and women love each other more. Doesn't that sound right? Then why do men and women find themselves more alone and isolated than ever? Why have men and women's communication skills become more and more difficult and confusing? Perhaps because instant gratification is not exactly the secret to making intimate relationships work.

Women are at their wits' ends trying to satisfy men in order to have one of them finally make good towards them, marry them, and create with them the family they have been yearning for. Even the most achieved career woman will eventually want to be a mother; not all of them, but most of them.

In their high career days, women did not think much of having lovers with whom they enjoyed spending time with, but would never want to marry. Yet, the years passed by and their biological clocks are now urging them to play for keeps. But how is this done? How do we play for keeps?

This book is about changing your thoughts about dating, and thus changing the outcome of your dating efforts.

I wrote this book to help you put into practice what I have learned and help you develop healthier attitudes towards men and dating. Hopefully, you will see noticeable, positive changes in the type of men you will attract. These new men in your life should reflect more the type of men you have been looking for and will open arrays of new and exciting dating experiences while moving towards your goal of finding a man you will want to marry.

With this book, you will be ready to start your journey in finding the life partner you have been dreaming of. For reinforcement, I also use pledges throughout the book. I find it a most efficient way to imprint one's brain with newly learned tools.

I want to take this opportunity to thank you for reading this book. I hope you will have as much fun reading it as I had researching for it and writing it. I am very happy to share these findings with you and I am looking forward to your comments. I wish you a most beautiful reading experience!

–Fléchelle Morin

Arthur & Yvonne

If you love somebody, let them go, for
if they return, they were always yours.
And if they don't, they never were...

Kahlil Gibran

ON A WARM NIGHT IN SEPTEMBER 1920, after a beautiful and enjoyable evening, Arthur and Yvonne stood at the front door of Yvonne's house, bidding good night to each other. Yvonne was smiling, obviously enamored, while Arthur held her hands. At fifteen years old, how could she not be spellbound by twenty-seven-year-old Arthur? He was charming, loving, fun, and easygoing. Moreover, he was a respected man in the community, and worked at the railroad company. Arthur was a catch.

They looked at each other intensely, aware of the hustle and bustle from the other inhabitants of the house. In those days, the houses front doors were enclosed, which made it a little more private.

Arthur leaned over to kiss Yvonne. Yvonne gently turned her head to let Arthur kiss her left cheek. Arthur retracted, looked at her, and asked for her permission to kiss her on her lips. Yvonne told him that she did not kiss anyone casually; she was to keep herself for the man who was to marry her.

Arthur, feeling rejected, told Yvonne that he would not court a woman who did not want to kiss him. Yvonne maintained her stance, and Arthur walked away into the night.

Arthur stopped calling upon Yvonne, and she was heartbroken.

19

Arthur was not accustomed to being refused affection from a woman. After all, he was quite a catch and he knew it. His thoughts turned towards his ex-fiancé. She kissed him the first time he asked her, all right. She was quite a beauty. She was smart and spirited. Spirited indeed, he remembered. Arthur had bought a house in town where they would live, have a family of their own and grow old together. He remembered how he surprised her by taking her there for the first time on a Sunday afternoon.

He had opened the front door and let her in. As he followed her in the house, she turned around, faced him, took his cigar from his mouth and threw it on the walkway that led to the house. She told him, "Arthur, you may smoke, but never in *my* house." Arthur remembered the moment he decided to walk away from her and their relationship. Arthur moved into the house by himself and set himself to find another wife.

Oh, yeah... Yvonne. She was the one who made him think about all this. Well, he was just going to walk away from her and keep looking for another woman. And look he did for the next couple of weeks. Yvonne's laughter and open heart made him ache, as his ego battled with him. His ex-fiancé had been kissing him, but she did not respect him. Yvonne respected herself and in turn, respected him. That's all it took for him to take a walk down the little street leading to Yvonne's house.

My grandparents were married on December 29, 1920, and my mother was born a year later.

The No Kissing Interview

Stewart: One of our guests this morning is Fléchelle Morin. Good morning Fléchelle, welcome to our show.

Fléchelle: Good morning.

Stewart: Former CEO turned Dating Specialist... What made you make that transition?

Fléchelle: A few years ago, I saw the business of dating as an emerging business for the future. I therefore decided to investigate this growing business and learn more about the dater's needs.

Stewart: What did you find out?

Fléchelle: I found that the dater's needs are pretty basic on the surface – What should I wear? Should I call her to confirm our dinner date? Should I call him to thank him for a great evening? However, deep down, daters need help with fundamental behavioral changes.

Stewart: Wow, what type of fundamental behavioral changes are we talking about?

Fléchelle: For example, for the women who are hearing their biological clocks ticking and are wanting to find a husband in order to start a family, I am helping them to first break their old dating habits, which have only taken them so far to short-lived casual relationships, and to embrace new and healthy dating practices.

21

If a woman wants to build a foundation to grow a long-term viable relationship with a man, she has to discipline herself (easier said than done), and stay focused on her goal. I help women get what they want and need from their relationships of choice with men.

Stewart: In your book *Kissing or No Kissing ~ Whom Will You Save Your Kisses For?*, you tell women they would do better not to kiss the frogs, and wait for their princes. Don't you think this is a little bit extreme in this day and age?

Fléchelle: Along with my suggesting that women stay clear of the frogs, I also tell them that it is okay to kiss the frogs if they want to, but to do it with a lucid mind; they should not lose sight that they are, in fact, only kissing a frog.

I am hoping to help women keep their focus on their wish to be married to a prince and stop fantasizing that the frog they have hooked up with might someday turn into one.

Stewart: Why is it bad for women to fantasize?

Fléchelle: It is bad for women to fantasize if they are in their mid-thirties and forties, and they want to be married and start a family. They have no time to lose. If they would have been more choosy in their twenties and early thirties, maybe they would now be married with a family of their own.

Stewart: So you are not exactly against kissing?

Fléchelle: No, not at all. I simply want women to keep the prospects of their goals even while rubbing elbows with the frogs. We all know a woman or two who have been dating the wrong guy for ten years or so and found themselves still single and far from being a member of the married club.

Stewart: Can you tell us more about the "No Kissing Plan?"

Fléchelle: The "No Kissing Plan" is like a diet for weeding out the wrong men. Not that they are wrong within themselves, but they are men who for whatever reason, do not want to marry and start a family in the allotted amount of time the woman has.

In kissing and cuddling, most women will start bonding to a man; any man, good or bad. By postponing kissing and cuddling, women have better chances to walk away from the men who are not on the same page they are. It weeds out the non-serious contenders.

Stewart: Okay, I understand. But how would a woman go about it? She simply tells a man "I am on the No Kissing Plan," or "I don't kiss men?"

Fléchelle: There are many ways a woman can let men know what she wants and needs before she gives herself and her kisses away. One of the ways I suggest women to go about this is to wait for the man to ask her for a kiss. Then, and only after the man has asked for it, can she tell him that she doesn't feel comfortable with casual kissing. Of course, the man is going to be taken aback. Most men today are being offered sex by women, or they are being asked if they're gay for not asking women to have sex by the third date. Usually, the man will ask her what she means by "casual kissing." I suggest women tell their dates that they are looking for a husband and simply do not feel comfortable kissing a man who is just a date. The man might ask her what she needs in order to feel comfortable kissing. Then she can tell him that being in a committed relationship leading to marriage with a formal engagement would make her feel safe enough that she is not kissing a frog! Most men have a good laugh at the "not kissing a frog" comment, especially if the woman keeps it light and breezy and has conviction in her beliefs. They'll go home thinking they have just met someone pretty special.

Stewart: Well, I have no doubt that you are onto something really interesting here, and I can't wait to see where it goes. Good luck with your book.

Fléchelle: Thank you.

· · ·

Part One

Getting Acquainted
~ The Basics

· · ·

1

What Is The "No Kissing Plan" And Why It Works

You may conquer with the sword, but you are conquered by a kiss.

Daniel Heinsius

YOU'VE ASKED ME, "WHAT IS THIS NO KISSING BUSINESS?" Some of you have told me that you haven't heard anything as backward as my "No Kissing Plan." Really? Want to try again?

What about "I don't know what happened! We started kissing, and from one thing to another, we were having sex!" Or the ever-popular one, "I could not say no. I could not stop myself…"

The "No Kissing Plan" is not about not kissing at all, it is about not kissing the wrong man for the wrong reason.

Have you ever kissed someone you did not really like, ended up in bed with him, and sat by the phone for weeks waiting for him to call? How many times did you have a casual affair turned into an obsession?

The "No Kissing Plan" is about *not* finding yourself in the wrong relationship with the wrong guy. It is about taking care of yourself first, while hunting and attracting the man you really want in your life. By keeping your head clear from the cloud of sexual satisfaction, you are free to make the right choices in your life. Most importantly, you need to understand that kissing a man won't make him fall for you; men do not marry women because they gratify them with their sex.

The "No Kissing Plan" is about kissing the right man after getting what you need and want from him first.

If what you want is a one-night stand, then go ahead and kiss anyone you want for that night.

If what you want is to be married, then I strongly suggest you not kiss anyone until he has given you a promise to investigate a married life with you, through the act of engagement by presenting you with a ring and his commitment to a future life leading to marriage for the two of you. Until you get this straightforward promise, you should keep dating others until one of your prospective contenders is serious enough to make it worthwhile for you to be taken off the market.

Without a ring you are not engaged. A promise to get a ring after he has test driven your body for "sexual compatibility," after his daughter is older, his mother dies, his ex-wife gets over him or when he has time to shop for one are only lame excuses not to give you what you need and want in order to give up your freedom from dating others and get you at the cheapest price possible for him. While starting your relationship right and getting a ring first is not a fail proof guarantee that you won't ever have your heart broken, at least you are one step farther than a verbal promise; actions speak louder than words. It has nothing to do with the size or the monetary value of the ring; it has to do with the commitment significance of being engaged and the feeling of being honored, which you will carry with you throughout the life of your relationship.

Other perks gained from following the "No Kissing Plan" include:

- Not getting bonded to a man who lied about his marital status. Many married men are posing as unmarried or divorced men who are dating in search

28

~~of a woman to marry.~~

- Not getting bonded to a man who is not ready to commit.

- Will allow you to choose your mate with your brain (intellectually), instead of with your body (chemically and emotionally). It will allow you to use reason over passion, therefore making better choices in regards to your love relationships (and possibly in many other areas of your life.)

- Not turning off good men who won't be able to handle your kissing the other men courting you.

Since you will be multiple dating in your search to find your future husband, do not kiss anyone. Men cannot handle the thought of another man's hands (even less his mouth) on the woman they consider marrying. Why risk losing the man who would be perfect for you because he thinks of another man's mouth on yours every time he kisses you? Do not kiss at all.

Besides, kissing is very intimate and powerful. A woman needs a lot of inner strength to keep a kiss from developing into something more.

Kissing a man will chemically bond you to him. Oxytocin is the bonding agent believed to be responsible for possibly most feelings of "love" we feel towards a stranger we might just have met and rubbed elbows with. Oxytocin is a neurohypophysial peptide that is released from the posterior pituitary gland and is distributed in the systemic circulation system. Oxytocin is a powerful hormone that is released through the action of touching, kissing, cuddling, and so on, and it will trick you into thinking you need to be with this man, no matter what. In the movie *It Started With A Kiss* (1959), Debbie Reynolds falls for Glenn Ford (the man she was not at all interested in) after he kisses her as an "experiment only..." Falling for a man after kissing him is nothing new!

Feelings of love and attachment, therefore, might be more the result of a chemical reaction starting in the brain than a matter of the heart. Keep that in mind next time you feel that you are falling for a man who hasn't yet proven to you that he is worthy of your devotion!

Although being chemically bonded to a good man is a most wonderful feeling and is good for both your physical and emotional health, being bonded to a man who hasn't promised you to seriously look into a future life together through the allegiance of an engagement is a very risky proposition. Being bonded to a man will make you feel and act as if you are in a committed relationship, but without a concrete commitment, what will you get? You might end up wasting more years of your precious life with a man who will end up walking away from you or drive you nuts enough for you to eventually leave on your own, leaving you disillusioned about love one more time. You cannot afford to lose any more time, especially if your goal includes having children and building a family.

The "No Kissing Plan" is easy:

- You only need to discipline your urges. It is like being on a diet from binging on casual meaningless sex, in exchange for a long-term meaningful relationship with a cherishing, loving, and caring man.

- Do not kiss a man until you get what you need and want first from him.

- Should you kiss a frog, just keep in mind that a frog is a frog, and keep dating others in order to meet your prince.

I promise, on my honor, that if I should kiss a frog, I won't try to change him into the prince he is not.
So help me God.

Of course, your kissing men won't ultimately keep you from getting married; it is just that adopting the "No Kissing Plan" will help you keep your head clear and will make it easier for you to move on from a man—no matter how sexy he is—who has no potential as a long-term mate for you. If you absolutely must kiss your date, I suggest at least to kiss all your dates so that you do not prematurely bond to any one of them before you get the commitment you need. Kissing multiple men will keep you from bonding too much to any of them, as oxytocin has a tendency to make people feel in love with the last person they kiss. This way, you'll feel in love with Paul on Monday, by Wednesday it will be Michael you'll want to marry, and by Saturday, Steve will hold your loving attention. At least this way you will not get in an imaginary daze with any of them and won't go into premature monogamy until you get a solid commitment from one of them.

Please keep in mind that if you kiss them, some of your dates won't be able to deal with the fact that you are multiple dating and might leave you just for that. You have to ask yourself, is it worth it? Believe me, there will be plenty of time to bond to the right man for you: a man who will want to be there for you tomorrow, and the day after, and the day after that. Again, marriage minded men do not mind waiting to have sex in order to end up with the right women for them; they know they can have plenty of good time women and value courting a virtuous one.

If you want to be married, follow my "No Kissing Plan." I promise you will find a good, marriage minded man in the next twelve months. Try it. What do you have to lose? If the way you have been dating works for you, keep doing it. If it no longer works and you think that you are ready to try something new, then put this program in practice today; it will work for you. Follow these simple steps and you will be married.

JUSTINE'S CASE:

Justine had been out of her last relationship for just over a year. It had not been an easy breakup, and she had promised herself to choose a better man next time. As she was going about her life, refusing to date anyone until she met the man she was looking for, she met Claude, a gregarious and personable business owner. He was not at all the man she was looking for, but he was nice and offered to spend time with her as friends only. She thought it would be a good way to spend some time doing fun things while still looking for her future mate.

They started going to movies, dinners and walks, and they spent a few nights a week in each other's company. One night, after watching a movie at his house and after a few glasses of wine, they started kissing, and then one thing led to another, and they ended up having sex together. She said that although she knew this was not the right thing to do, it felt good and she was ready to have a lover while waiting for Mister Right to show up.

Although there were plenty of things she didn't like about him, along with the fact that he was only half decent in bed, he was conveniently there. She trusted that even if she enjoyed Claude's company, she would not fall for him as he was an unsuitable mate for her.

Within a few weeks she said that she started to have codependent behavior towards Claude. She started to feel jealous of his other female friends, whom he said were only friends just like her. She also quickly realized that he was free to have sex with any of them, and it drove her totally crazy. She started to invite him every night to do something with her, and it would kill her when he would cancel a night with her to spend it with another one of his female friends.

Justine ended up spending a year and a half in this dead end relationship. She was with a man who was not there for her—a man she did not even want for herself in the first place. Claude enjoyed having her being part of his harem, even if it meant having to deal with her when she would come to his house in the middle of the night and bang the door until he had to let her in so as not to disturb his neighbors. Justine was totally chemically bonded to Claude. As with any other addiction, when she finally got the strength to walk away from him and stop seeing him, she started to feel better about herself. She was almost fully recovered from this ordeal one-and-a-half years later. Justine paid a high price for kissing Claude that night and thinking that she was able to handle having sex with a man without falling for him.

· · ·

2

What Personality Type Are You?

> *The art of being yourself at your best*
> *is the art of unfolding your personality*
> *into the person you want to be. . . .*
> *Be gentle with yourself, learn to love*
> *yourself, to forgive yourself, for only*
> *as we have the right attitude toward*
> *ourselves can we have the right*
> *attitude toward others.*
>
> Wilferd A. Peterson

FINDING AND UNDERSTANDING YOUR PERSONALITY TYPE is very important. You need to discover your personality type in order to attract the right type of man for you. You might like your type or want to change it and become another type, which is fine, but first you need to find what personality type you are, easily analyze it, and get the tools needed to work with your personality type or to change your type for the desired one. Read the following statements to find out to which type group you belong.

IN A RELATIONSHIP YOU ARE THE FEMININE TYPE IF:

- You like men and enjoy receiving from them.

- You enjoy a man who is in charge and makes decisions for you both.

- You feel at ease with a man who cherishes your feelings.

- You instinctively want to respect good men.

- You don't want to stay with bad men in order to fix them.

- You feel right at home with a man who protects you and will put himself in the face of danger to make sure you are safe.

- You enjoy doing things for men to show them your appreciation in regards to their generosity towards you.

- You enjoy being pampered and have no problem saying yes, please and thank you to men's offerings when it doesn't make you feel uncomfortable.

- You have no problem saying no when something makes you feel uncomfortable.

- You put yourself first and take care of yourself, and your needs.

IN A RELATIONSHIP YOU ARE THE MASCULINE TYPE IF:

- You like to get into debates with men and like to show off your knowledge.

- You like to win, and competition with your man is a turn-on.

- You like to protect and cherish the man of your life.

- You are self-sufficient and can take care of yourself and your man.

- You like to take care of your man's feelings and make sure he feels good about himself and the relationship.

- You like to lead the relationship.

- You like to have a partner who is willing to follow your lead.

- You enjoy being generous with your time, money, and energy towards your man.

- You feel good when your man respects your leadership and it makes you feel even more lovable towards him when he respects your direction choices.

In your relationships you are both male and female if you answered yes to most of the above statements. Alpha females have a balance of both energies. However, in a relationship where you will be sharing time and space with a man, you will have to pick the predominant energy you'll want to be; you cannot be both. If you want more detailed information about this subject, I recommend reading Dr. Pat Allen and Sandra Harmon's books *Getting To "I Do"* and *Staying Married And Loving It. Why Men Don't Listen and Women Can't Read Maps* from the husband and wife team Allan and Barbara Pease is another good book you might want to read.

It is very important that you choose the type of woman you want to be in your marriage, as narcissism has no place in a relationship that takes into account the wants, needs and feelings of both people. In order to make a relationship work between two people, one needs to be the male energy and the other one the female energy. Both partners need to be complementary to each other.

If you are a feminine energy woman, then you need to attract the opposite energy, which is the male energy, in order to complement yourself in a relationship. If you are a masculine energy woman, you need to find a feminine energy male to compliment you.

Leader types, competitive types, heads of teams and controlling types are masculine energy types. They make suitable complementary partners for feminine energy women.

Creative and artistic types and followers are feminine energy types. These creative feminine yin types make perfect mates for the strong, competitive, controlling type of women. With such a woman, feminine yin types are led into action in their relationship. If these feminine types were to choose a feminine energy woman as a mate, both partners would offer no relationship direction, and stagnation would soon set to the detriment of both partners.

The same disparity occurs if a masculine energy woman chooses a masculine energy man to have a relationship with. Very rarely will a masculine man want to settle down with a masculine energy woman, since men do not want to be challenged in their love relationships; they have enough challenges at work. The relationship between both yang partners would be competitive, as both would want to lead and control the flow of the relationship and would want to sit in the king's chair. And unfortunately, there is only one "king's chair." In a loving relationship, both partners sit side by side in their respective king and queen's chair, not on top of each other.

Alpha females and alpha males can also create a good balance of energy in their relationship as long as they switch their energy to complement their mate's energy. When the alpha male is acting out from his masculine energy, the alpha female needs to be acting from her feminine energy. When the alpha male is acting out from his feminine energy, the alpha female needs to be acting from her masculine energy. Both the alpha partners need to be complementary to each other in order to maintain the productive energy flow of the relationship.

As I mentioned earlier, this book was written especially for women who have chosen to be the yin feminine energy in their relationship of choice. As you will learn more about yourself and the personality and energy type that fits you best, you will act in a more responsible and loving manner in all your relationships.

3

Choosing Your Non-Negotiables

*The art of being happy lies in the power of
extracting happiness from common things.*

Henry Ward Beecher

CAROLINE: "FOR ME, ONE OF MY NON-NEGOTIABLES is that a man
needs to be extremely intelligent—brilliant, in fact…"

Non-negotiables in selecting a mate are things, behavior and/or
aspects you cannot live with or without. Because men, same as
women, are far from being perfect, I suggest keeping your non-
negotiables list to a minimum. Try to keep your list as short as
three non-negotiables. In fact, if you can live with only one or
two, the better.

What is a non-negotiable? How should I decide what non-
negotiables I need? How do I differentiate between a non-
negotiable and a "want"?

A non-negotiable is something that you know at the bottom of
your heart and in the depth of your soul is a requisite quality in the
man you will allow to court you. For example, non-negotiables
for a woman could be that a man must be drug free, at least six
feet tall, healthy, wealthy and kind.

Be aware that by being extra demanding on the qualities your
man should have, you are limiting yourself. Realize that your
need for him to be at least six feet tall is mostly a "want," rather

than a non-negotiable, and should not be considered as a non-negotiable, unless, of course, you can make it fit into your three non-negotiables list.

If one of your non-negotiables is that a man would need to love your twelve cats, two dogs and four birds (good for you if you find a man who would accept and love all your animals), keep in mind the reality that many men do not care about having animals roaming around the house, and unless you can be flexible about your animals, you might end up raising more cats and dogs than babies!

So be flexible about all your non-negotiables. If your list of non-negotiables looks like "He needs to be intelligent, caring, loving, affectionate, spend lots of time with me, make lots of money, take time off from work to go to Daddy and Me at school with our future kids, do the dishes and tell me that I am beautiful every day, then I would say you have more things to worry about than finding a husband.

Next, make a list of your non-negotiables. Actually, write them down on a sheet of paper; a list in your head won't do. Your first list will include all the non-negotiables you can think of. When you are done making this list—take your time, it might take you a day or two—then take another sheet of paper and copy only the most important half of the non-negotiables written on the first list. This becomes your second list. When you are done with this task—again make sure you take your time—start with a third sheet of paper and do the same thing you did with the previous one; copy only half of the non-negotiables. This list becomes your third list. Continue doing this until you have no more than three non-negotiables.

Now, take your last list and write beside it the names of the boyfriends, lovers and husbands you have had who met your non-negotiables. Chances are just a few, if any, would make that list, right? You are on your way to meet a totally different type of man—a type of man you haven't met yet. Are you starting to be excited now? We create our own realities, and when we become aware and take responsibility for our actions, we see lots of beautiful changes and growth in our lives.

You will now know that if a man does not fit your requirements, it has nothing to do with him; it has to do with you and the choices you make in your life.

If you keep saying about your dates: "He doesn't meet my non-negotiables," then perhaps it is time for you to renegotiate your non-negotiables, right? What do you think? You have to make sure that your non-negotiables do not surpass the capabilities of men. If not, it can only mean a new title for you: "Eternally Single." Remember, you are in charge of your own destiny.

I promise, on my honor, to choose attainable non-negotiables in order not to remain single for the rest of my life. So help me God.

Which takes us now to the next chapter, "*Making And Keeping Commitments.*"

· · ·

4

Making And Keeping Commitments

*There are no enduring successes unless
commitments are made and kept.*

HOPEFULLY BY NOW YOU HAVE FOUND THE ENERGY TYPE you are
or want to be, and have decided that you will date a few different
types of men in order to figure out which type would work best
for you.

Making and keeping commitments to yourself are very
important steps in finding and keeping the right man for you.
Making and keeping commitments to yourself will allow you to
take responsibility for your actions, keep you on track and help
you reach your goal.

If you really want to marry, then make a commitment to date
only eligible men. By eligible men, I mean men who are not
already married, men who are not eternally narcissistic, men who
are not still "thinking" about getting married although they have
been thinking about it for the last twenty years, or men who are
not currently in jail and will be for the next thirty years.

An eligible man is a man who portrays himself as single and
emotionally available with the desire to create a partnership with
a woman. Of course, this is a short list of what an available man
is; they come in many different formats, but I think you get the
point.

Although dating separated men is great practice in order for you to learn how to act feminine on a date, just know that separated men are further from making a marriage commitment to a woman than a man who is already divorced or single.

Of course, you will have to date a man at least three times or more before knowing what is the availability of that man. Simply use good judgment in deciding to spend a fair amount of time with a man without knowing if he is eligible or not.

Write down on a sheet of paper the commitments you are ready to make and keep. You will need to re-read them if you start feeling weak about your commitments.

If one of your non-negotiables is not to be married to a man who heavily drinks alcohol or uses recreational drugs, then make the commitment to yourself that you will no longer date a man who has inebriated himself to the point of not being able to drive a vehicle or a man who tells you he needs to smoke marijuana in order to relax at night before falling asleep.

If one of your non-negotiables is to be married to a man who is ready to have children with you, then make the commitment to yourself that you will stop dating this great guy who just announced to you that he had a vasectomy fifteen years ago and having children would be totally out of the question.

If one of your non-negotiables is to marry a man who is kind and protective, make the commitment to yourself that you won't be dating this most gorgeous fellow you met while skiing, because he is belligerent towards women.

Get it? Men appreciate and value a woman who can make commitments and values herself enough to keep them. Bad boys will spend lots of time and energy trying to make a good woman trip and fall; good women are a challenge for them. Good men also will try to make you fall, but in their cases, they do it because they need to make sure that you are as virtuous as you say you are.

Carmen is the subject of our next story. Carmen had made a self-commitment to marry a good man and had decided that she would not be intimate with any man until he had given her a commitment with a formal engagement, a ring and a wedding date. Carmen was committed to the promise she made to herself, and her vigilance paid off.

CARMEN'S CASE

Carmen was actively dating when she met Mitch. Mitch was all that a beautiful woman such as Carmen was looking for. He was good looking, successful, owned a beautiful house, and his words were music to her ears. Soon after starting to date her, Mitch told Carmen that at forty-two years old, he was looking to be married to a traditional woman such as her. He said he appreciated her wanting to keep herself for her future husband and would be happy to wait in order to have such a woman in his life. Mitch asked Carmen to see him exclusively as he was really close to making up his mind about getting married. He felt that the two of them being in an exclusive relationship would help him make up his mind about moving forward in becoming a married man—a man married to her.

Although Carmen felt it would be better for her to keep her options open and continue dating until engaged, she decided to take a calculated risk: She stopped seeing her other suitors and started an exclusive, non-intimate relationship with Mitch.

As the weeks passed by, Mitch tried to convince Carmen that it would be okay for her to be intimate with him as he was so close to making the decision to marry her and that they were certainly both old enough to handle being in an intimate relationship. Carmen kept her commitment to herself and kept repeating that although she felt really good with him and that she was extremely attracted to him, she did not feel comfortable starting an intimate relationship before he honored her with the formal commitment she needed, as she would feel prematurely married to him. Carmen had the same conversation with him at least a dozen of times.

One night Carmen was out with a girlfriend having a drink at a local hotel lobby when she saw Mitch walk in with two of his buddies. Mitch was very surprised to come face to face with

Carmen, but he accepted Carmen's invitation to join her and her girlfriend. Carmen and her girlfriend were not oblivious to the disappointment of Mitch's friends and kept their eyes open when one of his friend abruptly excused himself and walked towards the door where three women had just walked in. One of the women hugged him and introduced the two other women to him. He made a gesture to suggest for them to go outside, and they left. Within a minute, Mitch's phone rang and after a fifteen-second exchange, Mitch said that it was his friend who did not want to be in that hotel anymore and had asked Mitch to meet him outside, as he wanted for them to go somewhere else.

After kissing her good night, he and his remaining friend left. Carmen and her girlfriend looked at each other and said nothing until Carmen told her girlfriend that she knew she had better be very vigilant with this man. They both left and had dinner at a nearby restaurant.

Carmen decided to look at Mitch's actions instead of listening to his words. She knew the three women who were in the hotel lobby that night were Mitch and his friends' dates and that Mitch had breached their exclusivity agreement.

Two days later, as they sat in front of the fireplace, Mitch surprised her with a little jewelry box. Inside was a ring—a sapphire and diamond ring. Mitch did not say anything and Carmen asked him what this ring represented. Mitch told her that she could call it a friendship ring or an engagement ring or whatever she wanted to call it. Carmen said thank you and asked him to put it on her finger. Mitch took the ring and put it on Carmen's middle finger, then asked her if they could now have sex. She thanked him for the ring and for his offer of lovemaking, but said that she was not feeling quite comfortable having sex with him just yet, that it was getting late, and it was time for her to go home.

The following weekend after a class, Carmen went to Mitch's house where it was agreed that she would take a shower and get ready for their dinner date while he was out shopping. Mitch had left the door unlocked, and Carmen walked in, stepping over a

"Playboy" magazine that had been left by the door on the floor.

As she was getting ready to get in the shower, she saw a condom wrapper and a feminine pad paper strip in the bathroom trash can. The trash can had been moved from under the sink to beside the toilet where it was more visible. Mitch lived alone. She looked at the feminine pad paper strip and it had been crumbled. No women crumble their feminine pad paper strip before throwing it in the trash she thought. She called her girlfriend and asked her what she would do with her feminine pad paper strip upon removing it from the feminine pad. Her girlfriend answered that she would put it in the trash. Carmen asked her if she would crumble it, and her friend said no. She asked Carmen why, and Carmen told her the story. Her friend confirmed what Carmen had thought—it was a plant. Mitch was trying to make her crazy and have her either leave him or put out.

Carmen decided to take her shower and get ready as planned. Mitch came home as she was finishing her last makeup touch up, and she saw him in the mirror stretching his neck to look into the trash can. She did not react to him, and decided to let him make his next move.

Mitch acted surprised that she still wanted to have dinner with him. In fact, he had made a reservation at an expensive restaurant, which was unusual for him, and upon hearing that they were still on for dinner, tried to change their plan to go to an inexpensive local restaurant. Carmen said that she was so disappointed as she had been looking forward to this very classy restaurant, and would it be possible for them to still go there?

Mitch obliged and was not in a very good mood that night. After the evening, he invited Carmen for a nightcap before she drove home. She accepted his offer and sat with him by the fireplace. She listened to his telling her that he was not going to wait for sex from her for much longer. Because Carmen had kept her head clear from the bonding effects of oxytocin, she saw through Mitch and all of his head games.

The day after she took the ring to a jeweler who told her Mitch probably paid around ten to fifteen dollars for this blue and clear glass, silver ring.

Carmen decided to let Mitch do the breaking up, even though he did everything possible to make her do it. He broke up with her three days later, telling her that she was a wonderful woman, but unfortunately, he did not think he was ready to commit to marriage. He was ready to commit to sex and have her commit her body and mind to him, but that was the extent of it. Carmen did the right thing by not having sex with him. Although she really liked him, she could very well have fallen into a six-month or more sex relationship with him. Mitch was very good looking and told Carmen, in fact, that she was the only woman who had not ended up having sex with him. Mitch will remember Carmen for a very long time.

Mitch was not a bad man; he was simply more interested in taking care of himself and his feelings than taking care of a woman's feelings. Of course, making Carmen, a virtuous woman, fall into his bed would have been great for his ego, but the reality is that Mitch was simply unable to honor Carmen and cherish her feelings, and that doesn't make for a good husband, wouldn't you say? The only thing Carmen would have acquired from Mitch would have been a broken heart, as he would have left her after tiring of having sex with her. Carmen acted upon Mitch's actions, not his words, and as we all know, actions speak louder than words. Carmen was very smart to keep her eyes and ears open.

Because she kept her head, heart and sanity intact, she right away was able to start looking for a solid potential mate. She met her future husband a few weeks later at an ice hockey game. And Mitch? Well, who cares?

5

Dating Budget

*An ounce of action is worth a
ton of theory.*

Ralph Waldo Emerson

WHAT IS A DATING BUDGET AND WHY DO I NEED ONE? A dating budget is how much you are ready to invest in order to find a mate for yourself.

You will invest time, money and energy in your quest to find a husband. Most importantly for a woman is to decide how much time she will invest in finding a husband. I know that most of you are extremely busy with work, friends and family. You are already overloaded with responsibilities, and you will have to make time for your dating endeavors.

First, lets talk about time. If you can afford to take time off to have dinner, then I would suggest you invest time in dinner dates. Let face it, you need to eat anyway, and dinner dates are a good way to multi task. On dinner dates, you eat and you learn about someone new. And while you eat, you won't talk as much, which is always a good thing. Do not miss an opportunity to keep quiet.

In order to be able to date a few nights a week, if you are very busy, I suggest you meet men in your own neighborhood. When scheduling dates with men, tell them you would prefer to meet them around where you live or work. Don't tell men "I do not date outside of my zip code," because you don't know where they are going to offer to take you to dinner; it might be to a restaurant you've always wanted to try, and you would gladly drive for that one special outing. I know a woman who told a man she would not meet him where he wanted to go because she had never heard of the restaurant, and it turned out it was one of the best in town. She is a very educated businesswoman, but I guess she did not know much about restaurants. So let him suggest a place. Most men will drive to meet you where you want to go. You might also just want to meet men for a drink at a place on the way from your work. I do not care much for drink dates as I do not find them intimate enough and because I like to spend quality time with a man, but if you absolutely cannot do otherwise, drink dates are better than no dates at all.

In your budget, write the amount of hours you are ready to dedicate to dating. Schedule at least two hours for dinner, and thirty to forty minutes for a drink date. You can even schedule a drink date at six o'clock at a local bar with one man, and dinner at seven with another man at a nearby restaurant. I personally find it quite tiring, but I know women who have strong constitutions enough to work that hard in their quest to find a husband.

Now, let's talk about money spent. Will you be dating on the Internet, or will you hire a personal matchmaker? A personal matchmaker is expensive but might be worth every dollar if you are a busy executive with limited time who can afford to pay the high price these services usually charges. If your budget is somewhat limited, you might want to sign up on some of the free online dating services and spend more money sitting at pricey restaurants where men go to socialize and have dinner. Go to restaurants where they serve dinner at the bar. You can sit at the bar and sip on a drink while smiling at the men around you. If you are too shy to go sit in a restaurant by yourself and are worried about what people might think of a woman sitting alone at a bar, just go and tell people who ask you that you are meeting a girlfriend who, of course, never shows up. Many women I know get invited to dinner on a regular basis that way. It is a great way to meet men and have a first date right then and there.

There are a lot of places you can go where you will not spend much money—bookstores, markets, museums and libraries are just a few examples. In some cities there are also free concerts and free single events. Whatever your money budget is, write it down and stay within your means.

Also budget for clothes, accessories and for the upkeep of your hair and nails. You do not need to look like a model; in fact, you do not even need to be pretty, but you must look clean and smell good. Really, most men care very little if a woman is gorgeous or average looking. Most men I know do not see the difference between a beauty queen and the girl next door, as long as she looks happy and smiles a lot.

Get a nice-smelling perfume if you do not already have one, and wear nice-fitting clothes. Have only one outfit (which I call the dating uniform) if you cannot afford many, but make sure it flatters you. Make sure your hair is trimmed and that your nails are polished. Some women do not want to go to nail salons for health reasons, however, you can manicure your nails at home and have them look nice and clean. Of course, if you think that you have a few pounds to lose, then others probably notice it too, so lose those pounds. There is no need to be as thin as a rail (most men I know tend to like a more voluptuous woman anyway), but try staying within your ideal weight as much as you can. When you go out to dinner, eat half your meal and have the other half wrapped to bring home. You can have it for lunch the day after, thereby keeping the caloric intake down. By the way, when you ask your date to have your meal wrapped to take home (I suggest you ask your date what you want and need and let him take care of you by being the middleman between you and the staff; men love this), tell him that you'll be thinking about him the next day while eating this delightful leftover food for lunch. He will be even more enthralled by you.

Your budget should stay simple and easy to manage. Keep a log of the time you spend on dates and the money you spend. Be flexible; you might want to add more time to your schedule as you will realize how much more fun dating is. I can assure you that if you keep dating fun and uncomplicated, that is what dating will be: fun and uncomplicated. And needless to say, men are *very* attracted to fun, happy and uncomplicated women. You will exude an irresistible sensuality, which will be very appealing to the masculine energy men you are trying to attract in your life.

This is about all you have to do in order to start dating. So go out there, look good, smell good, be happy, and smile a lot.

PART TWO

RE-MAPPING YOUR BRAIN

6

Is It Human? Date Anybody and Anything With a Heartbeat

Success is a science; if you have the conditions, you get the result.

Oscar Wilde

WE ALL WANT TO DATE GEORGE CLOONEY OR Denzel Washington. The problem with this is that there is only one of each, so the chances for us to end up marrying one of them are pretty slim, wouldn't you say?

The premise of *Kissing Or No Kissing ~ Whom Will You Save Your Kisses For?* is finding a husband. Therefore, you cannot use the excuse of "Well, he is not George Clooney…"

I promise, on my honor, to date anything that has a heartbeat, no matter how much I need to lobotomize my brain. So help me God.

Date anybody who asks you out. Why wouldn't you? What do you have to lose? You need to be out there; you need to be seen; you need to be found. Any questions about that?

I hear women everyday saying things like "I don't want to go out with him, because he is too short" or "I don't want to accept a date with him, because he doesn't make enough money." So what if he is too fat, too skinny, too tall, too whatever. Who cares? You are not going to marry that man on that night! You should be thankful that a man—any man—asks you out, so that you can practice your dating skills.

Women have such high expectations that it is almost impossible for men to compete with their idealistic notions about happiness. The media has done a good job at making women feel bad about their body images for years, but even more damaging are the unreasonable expectations sold by the cliché "you can have it all," which makes women set standards for men that are unrealistic. He needs to be tall, have a body to die for, a full head of dark curly hair, and why not add "sparkling green eyes!"

A man can be tall and bald, or short with full a head of hair, or short and bald. Which one of these men will hold your hand during hardship in your life? All of them would, if they were just given a chance to provide for a woman. Women who believe that they can only be seen with good-looking men are narcissistic. They are also non-committable and use the excuse of body and face flaws so they do not have to commit to a man. And women also use this excuse to stay with men they know they should not be with. Get real. There are some things deeper than surface skin.

Unless you change your ways of thinking in regards to mate selection, you are going to keep doing the same thing over and over, and I think we would be right to say that the way you have done in the past did not work for you and won't work better in the future. Right?

Practicing your dating skills is a must in your search for the right husband for you. How would you know what type of man is good for you, if you have not gone out with many types of men? When people ask me what my type of man is, I answer, "The loving, cherishing, protective, marrying kind of guy." Not "Tall, dark hair, slim but muscular..." Really... What a waste of time.

Dating different types of men will allow you to grow personally and will help you make better choices in your love life. We are all attracted to the same type of man our last lover was; if he was short and bulky, this is what we seem to be attracted to after this romance is over.

So ladies, please get real about the man you will end up marrying. You have no way to know until you give multiple men a fair chance to impress you. Set your expectations at a reachable level for men. Not only will these men be happy to have the chance to take a beautiful Goddess such as you out on great dates, but you will also do yourself a favor to be out with men who want you instead of men you had to chase down the block in order for them to give you the short time of a coffee break. Get it?

·   ·   ·

Here Anne's letter in which she complains about this very subject:

Dear Fléchelle,
I am forty-two years old and have never been married. I am really getting discouraged because the men I like don't ask me out, and the ones who ask me out are the ones I don't want. How can I get the men I want to notice me, and keep the ones I don't want at bay? Anne

Dear Anne,
Your solution might not be in whom you want but in whom you actually need. Have you thought that perhaps it would be a good idea to start dating the men who want you instead of staying on the shelf for the ones who obviously do not want you? Perhaps you are setting your sights too high. You are no longer a twenty-year-old woman, and I would suggest you get real about what you have to offer to a man; perhaps what you have to offer does not match what the men you want are looking for. You are forty-two years old and you want to be married. Starting today, date the men who want you. You might be surprised that the men who want you

might be better deals for you than the ones *you* want. Give the chance to the men who are interested in you the opportunity to impress you. Good luck!

7

Multiple Dating: Why and How

We are what we repeatedly do. Excellence,
then, is not an act, but a habit.

Aristotle

MOST WOMEN WILL GO OUT ON A DATE, and if the man is nice to
them, they think that it automatically means that they both are
investigating a future together, which means she is concentrating
on this man only, and he, on her. Why would he not be interested
in seeing only her? Isn't she the complete woman any man would
be happy with? Wrong! Men do not "automatically" enter into an
exclusive, committed relationship, even if they have sex with a
woman regularly.

Multiple dating keeps the reality of dating in perspective. It
keeps women from over-fantasizing on a particular man before
he has had the chance to give her the commitment she needs and
wants. Dr. Allen calls it "Duty Dating"—quite a catchy name.

When you date multiple men, you open the door to multiple
opportunities in your life. Instead of waiting by the phone for
this one guy you met and you liked who has probably lost your
phone number after the fifteen minute talk you had with him at
the bar last weekend, you will be dining out and being treated like
a princess by a few or many interested and interesting gentlemen.
You will become more interesting yourself, as you will date

different types of men and expand your horizons by going to many different places. You might even be traveling to distant countries and learning about other cultures and ways of life while dating charming, intelligent, caring and generous gentlemen. You will be more attractive and mysterious to a man with whom you will enjoy yourself with than you would be by trying to impress this "one" guy you are trying to catch. Being the prey is a much better position to be in for a feminine woman than being the hunter.

Men will be drawn to your *je ne sais quoi* charms and will be enchanted by you. Therefore, expect to have your door bell rung by more flower deliveries than ever before. You'll enjoy moving your bouquet arrangements from one room to the next. Tonight's date is with Jay? Then you will set Jay's bouquet in the living room and Daniel and Henry's bouquets in the bedroom; tomorrow night's date is with Henry? Then you will set Henry's bouquet in the living room and Daniel and Jay's bouquets in the bedroom. Can you see how much fun this will be?

Look at dating as if interviewing in order to get a job as a wife.

Whether you are looking to be formally married or to be in a long term committed relationship, your goal will be more easily reached (on the emotional level at least) if you diversify by dating many men in order not to get too attached to one man (remember oxytocin?) before he commits to you, first by giving you what you require (ring and commitment to be in an engaged relationship leading to marriage, or a commitment to be exclusive in a long term relationship) in order for you to give your body and your "heart" to him. I find it wiser for a woman to obtain what it is she needs first before she starts feeling feelings of love for a man. Easier said than done!

Multiple dating will allow you to get to know men without fixating on one man only. You will find that you will get much less attached to one man in particular when you multiple date many men. You will get less attached to the men you date because multiple dating acts as an antidote to oxytocin, which, as you know by now, is a most powerful bonding agent. Oxytocin is like a drug, which under its influence will have you do things you would not normally do, such as prematurely become monogamous with a man who hasn't committed himself to you or become fixated on an unsuitable man for you.

Multiple dating won't have you saying "Why do I love him, he is not even nice to me?" Multiple dating will reduce the craving to be with "that" man, talk to "that" man, and think only of "that" man. These are all feelings you will feel when under the influence of oxytocin and the bonding it creates when you are around only "that one" man, smell only "that one" man, and date only "that one" man. How many years have you already lost thinking about men who were not there for you and are not in your life today?

Another very tangible perk you will get from multiple dating is the fact that you will entice men's natural desire to chase a woman. If you are at home waiting for "his" phone call, tell me why he should be rushing to call you? He knows you are waiting, which gives him the incentive to go out and chase other women. He doesn't have to make a rushed decision about you in order not to lose you; he knows he already has you. When you'll be busy and happily going on about your life, filling out your dance card to the topmost, he will want to chase you. And when he'll be chasing you, he'll be too busy chasing others, and even if he does, it's you he'll be thinking of. Get it?

And think of it this way: How does having dinner out a couple of times a week with men eager to please you sound? Yes, pretty good indeed.

Multiple dating while being on my "No Kissing Plan" will put you at the center of attention of all men you will allow to date you. You will be and feel much more attractive to the men you will go out with when you don't have puppy eyes at the end of the evening and are asking questions such as, "When will you call me again?" You will have a fun and light attitude that will make him want to see more of you real soon. These are only a few of the many benefits you will gain from multiple dating and following my "No Kissing Plan."

A woman who multiple dates and keeps her head clear by

following my "No Kissing Plan" finds it much easier to make a final decision when it comes to accepting a man's proposal of marriage. By taking her time while multiple dating, she has gotten to know a man as a potential long-term mate instead of a sex buddy that might or might not end up being there for her in the long run. She might even receive counter-offers from other suitors upon learning that someone else has taken her off the market. No man likes to think of his future wife living with someone else! And believe me, men always remember the "one that got away." Not that you will care when you'll be married to the man you will have made a reality in your life.

Multiple dating is somewhat like being on an auction floor: the more people who want what the auctioneer is selling, the higher the price. The more "out there" and in demand you are, the more valuable you will become. So do not be afraid that the one suitor you like the most will leave you after finding out that you are seeing other suitors. While I do not suggest that you put in their faces the fact that you are dating others until formerly engaged, you have nothing to hide if they ask you directly if you are seeing others. If asked—and only then—you may answer with a surprise intonation in your voice, something like: "Well, of course, darling. I am looking for a husband!" When men hear a logical answer such as that, they accept it. Your suitors will think, "Of course, she is smart not to sell herself short" and then will start thinking how much you are worth to them and if they can afford to take you off the market themselves. No need to give long-winded explanations. Keep it short and sweet. The less said the better.

Until you have an engagement ring on your finger, you are a single woman going on about your life. If they insist on your giving details, ask them if they are proposing to you. You can say: "Well Bill, I am flattered that you inquire about my single life. As you know, I am looking for a husband and until I find one, I'll keep myself available for a good man to find me and take me off the market with a ring and a formal engagement leading to marriage. Are you proposing to me, by any chance?" And then, let them think and talk. They might not be able to utter any comprehensible words for a little while, so take that time to smile and sip on your drink. Keep on dating, yours is out there!

You will have a great time while dating as long as you do not take it or them seriously, unless THEY are serious about YOU and act on their sincerity towards you with making you the woman of their lives. Until then, they are only practice.

I discuss in Chapter Ten, entitled "When To Give Exclusivity ~ The Talk," what you will need to get in order to give exclusivity to that very special man.

PATRICIA'S CASE

Patricia was in her late thirties when she heard my advice about multiple dating. She is not a particularly pretty woman and would be considered quite plain. A few pounds overweight with large hips, she doesn't fit the model type we see in magazines. She's always been somewhat shy and—being addicted to beauty and fashion magazines—felt even more inadequate.

She had a hard time getting a date and could not even imagine dating more than one man at a time. How could she have more than one man interested in her? It seemed that the only guys interested in her were always on the rebound from another relationship, or out of a job, or in some other bad predicament.

The first time I met Patricia, she seemed needy and clingy. She wanted so much to be in a relationship that her body language was saying, "I'll take anyone, please just love me!" She complained about being twenty pounds overweight for the last ten years and hated her body. Knowing that lots of generously proportioned women are married and happy, I knew that her weight had little to do with her not having a man in her life.

I first suggested for her to start an exercise program, start losing the weight she did not want, and get a new haircut (even if that meant going to a new hairdresser). Also, she could go to a department store in order to get a free makeup lesson offered by many makers of beauty products and get the new makeup they suggested. Then I told her she had to look at herself in the mirror every chance she got, smile and out loud tell herself how alluring and lovely she was.

Then she was going to shop for a dating uniform—one dress or pant suit that would be up-to-date and would look sexy while being classy, a few complimentary blouses or knit tops, new shoes and new accessories. This outfit would be her dating uniform. She would be wearing her uniform for six nights in a row and after that, at least three nights a week while out in bars, lobbies of large hotels, restaurants and everywhere she would be seen by men. And, most importantly, she would be wearing a large and inviting smile.

On her first night out, she had two men asking for her phone number. Two men who looked nice, employed and happy. Wow! That was novel for Patricia. She was very nervous and giggled a lot. At the end of the evening, she went home a winner. I had instructed her to get an answering device to get calls from all the men she would meet, and out again she went the following night.

At the end of the six nights, Patricia would walk into any venue feeling and looking like a star. Looking popular is an attitude. If you think you are a Goddess, then you are a Goddess. If you think you are nothing, then you are nothing.

When I saw Patricia again, she looked nothing like the pitiful woman I had first met. She was transformed into a beautiful woman and was ready to conquer the world. Men liked her aura and she attracted better and better men the more practice she got.

·   ·   ·

Here's Angelina's letter, which supports the fact that multiple dating is not a deterrent for good men. Real men not only like to chase, they need to chase. They like the excitement of competition, and they like to win. They need it as much as they need to breathe. Of course, I am talking about the masculine leader type, the "in charge" type of man, the go-getter, the pursuer, the type of man who will not fade away at the thought of taking on the responsibilities that marriage and a family will bring.

Dear Fléchelle,

I am following your dating advice and am dating multiple gentlemen. It is working very well for me and I feel clearer about what I want and don't want in a man.

Through the ups and downs of dating, I find that the men I am attracted to do not want me and the ones I do not want chase me non-stop. What is happening? I am clearly letting the ones I want know that I like them and that I am looking forward to hearing from them again. I am really starting to be discouraged, and I am thinking that I will never find a man for me to marry and have a family with. I feel really sad; please help. Angelina

Dear Angelina,

So you have realized that only the ones we are NOT interested in are running after us? And it doesn't make any sense for you, right? I understand why you would feel this way, but this is the reality for so many single women these days. The modern woman sees nothing wrong about asking men out or telling them up front they will say yes if they call them again.

I cannot stress it enough: Men love to chase. When you are *too* interested in a man, and *want* a man too much before he has had the chance to want you first, he senses it and won't chase you because he doesn't have to; he already has you. That is why the ones chasing are the ones you are not interested in; they are the only ones you allow to chase you because you are not waiting at home for them. The truth is that if the lady is too easy to get, then she is not worth it. Men value what they have to work hard for. And they want to chase, chase, and chase.

I am not telling you to treat the men you want as if you do not like them. You can signal your interest in them by being enchanting and pleasant, but do not tell them at the end of the evening that you cannot wait to see them again, or that you will be waiting for their phone call. Men will think there is something wrong with you if you are not busy being chased by others.

You can tell men that you enjoy their company and that you are appreciative of what they do for you. The rest of the time, light and breezy conversations about the "brilliance of Mars these days" are in order. Be responsive and available, charming and lovely.

Make sure that your dating calendar is filled to the maximum; it will keep you from fixating on any one man only. Just make openings when your number one calls; do not keep open slots for him. You can always cancel another date if he calls you with a better offer.

Practice makes perfect. Practice dating as much as you can and beautiful things will happen to you, I promise. Just relax and have fun. When the man who is yours shows up, you'll be ready and will know what to do.

I promise, on my honor, that I will date more than one man at a time in order not to get too attached to any one of them until I am formally taken off the market.
So help me God.

8

Double Booking,
Triple Booking

Luck is what happens when
preparation meets opportunity.

Lucius Annaeus Seneca

BECAUSE YOU WANT TO BE MARRIED, I find that resorting to "double booking" may help you stay on top of things when it comes to guaranteeing the best husband you can get. While not ensuring it, double booking will help you to be out there dating even if one or two men cancel your date at the last minute.

In my years of dating, I found that men canceled more dates with me than I ever did with them. I would sometimes have four dates scheduled for a Saturday night and go out with one of them without needing to cancel the others. Why? Because they canceled first. From "I have to take my daughter to her school dance," to "I have to take my dog to the vet," to "I think I am getting the flu," to "My car just broke down," I think I have heard all the excuses in the world. One called the restaurant we were meeting at to cancel our date after I had been already waiting for him for fifteen minute because his dog bit him… that afternoon! Right! I decided to stay and have dinner at the bar and met a charismatic gentleman who not only treated me to dinner that night, but also went on to take me out on many fabulous dates all around town. You never know whom you will meet while out on a date!

If you are one of the millions of women over the age of thirty years old today looking for a husband in order to have children, I think it would be safe to say that you have much time to lose by staying home on a Saturday night because a man you had a scheduled date with decided he had something better to do. Wouldn't you agree?

We need to keep a very open and loving heart in order not to hurt anyone's feelings in the process. You are not double booking your dates in order to hurt them but to ensure your lineage survival and get the best possible genes for the creation of your future children—somewhat like what is known as "the survival of the fittest."

Therefore, you have to do the BEST YOU CAN in order to hook the best man for you. You deserve a suitable man, and by being open and available when a good man calls you, even if he calls at the last minute, you will have better chances to get married.

.   .   .

Upon reading the "double booking" advice I gave to Madeleine, Tracy wanted to share her views with me. Following is Madeleine's letter and my answer, which prompted Tracy to share her disagreement with me.

Dear Fléchelle,
I meet many of my dates through Internet dating sites and am having a problem with men who cancel our dates at the last minute. By then, I have refused other men's invitations, and I find myself sitting at home alone on Saturday nights. I am so upset...

How can I minimize the risk of missing the opportunity to have a date with a man because I gave my evening to another one who ended up canceling our date? Madeleine

Dear Madeleine,
Since you are generating dates from Internet dating sites with

many different men whose reliability you know nothing about, your concern is entirely valid.

My suggestion to you is to "double book." That means that you have two scheduled dates on Saturday night; one date is at 7 PM with Paul at a French restaurant, and the other one, at 7 PM with Steve at an Italian restaurant. If they both call and confirm, cancel the one you like the least, let's say Paul, by saying something like: "I am sorry to have to cancel our plan, but I have to take care of a sick girlfriend. Can we reschedule?" Apologize, and book him for another night. Now, let's say that Mike (your ultimate number one man) calls on that Saturday afternoon (he is just back in town after closing a big business deal) and says that he would just love to see you... What will you do? Call Steve, and tell him the "girlfriend" story. Apologize and book him for another night. Go out with Mike and have a great evening. This is called "taking care of yourself." Good luck.

Immediately after reading my advice to Madeleine, Tracy wrote to me. Here's an extract of her letter along with my point by point answers to her questions:

To "Double Book" or not...

Dear Fléchelle,

I really respect your insights, but I have to tell you that I do not agree with your "double booking" advice. I want to share my thoughts with you and I am looking forward to your comments.

Tracy: I would feel bad to cancel a date with a man on short notice in order to go out with another man just because I think that this one might end up being a better deal.

Fléchelle: You have every right to want to take care of a man's feelings, however, a feminine woman takes care of herself first.

Tracy: How would your friend feel if you would cancel on him or her?

Fléchelle: If my friend is a real friend, he or she will understand

69

that I am looking for a husband, and that I need to make it my life priority for it to happen. If you want to be married, open your calendar for "that masculine man!" After you are married, dear, you'll have plenty of time to visit with your friends, especially if you are marrying a hot shot who works a lot.

Tracy: How would you feel if a man canceled on you to go out with another woman?

Fléchelle: Men do it to us all the time "I have to work late tonight..." And no, I would not feel bad if a man did it to me because I would have scheduled another date for that same night... So if a man canceled me at the last minute, I would not be upset at him, and I could even afford to be light and breezy with him (if he ever calls back) because I went out and had a good time with another man after he last canceled on me. Does that make sense to you?

Tracy: How can I make it okay to cancel my previous engagements with men?

Fléchelle: Because you do not want to turn down your potential future husband by telling him that you are busy when, in reality, you would be out with another man whom you know has low potential to make it to the altar with you.

Tracy: And can you imagine the terrible consequences that could come out from such a deceit?

Fléchelle: Oh, like what? Having two men fight over you? What happened to romanticism? I cannot think of anything more flattering than having two men fight over a woman! Would you not think it fascinating if you were sitting at a restaurant, and the woman sitting at the next table on a date had another man come to her and ask what she's doing? Until a woman has an engagement ring on her finger (or is in a committed relationship), she is a single woman going on about her life. If a man wants a woman to be committed to him, he had better be seriously committed to her.

Tracy: I think that keeping our commitments means that we would not cancel a date with a man on short notice for another man, just because the latter one could be a better deal in the future.

Fléchelle: Unless you are *seriously* looking for a husband...

Tracy: If a man doesn't cherish my feelings enough to early reserve my time, do you really think it is a good idea to give in and see him anyway?

Fléchelle: If he is calling you at the last minute because he has just finished a big merger with another public company, and he could not think of anybody else he would like better to celebrate than with you, then, of course, you should be there, looking more beautiful than ever.

Tracy: In reality, don't you think that men would see you as being so desperate to free yourself without prior notice or worse, that you have so little concerns about your friends that you would cancel them on a whim for a date with a man?

Fléchelle: Dearest, if the guy you have a date scheduled with for next week finds a better deal than you before then, believe me, he is not going to miss a better deal based on principles. Let's get real here. Besides, men don't think like that; they just think they are really lucky that you had no plans for that evening. After all, a Goddess like you is NEVER desperate!

Tracy: I think that changing our plans for a man would make him think less of us.

Fléchelle: Life is too short to let anybody's opinion of you change your course of actions. I would suggest you DO NOT tell the man you are out with that you canceled another one for him either. You do not owe him any explanation, dear.

Tracy: I think that we should always keep the plans we have previously made.

Fléchelle: Yep, that's how a lot of people pass on better deals...

Tracy: I think the best way to handle this matter is to say yes to the first invitation that we like, and say no to the rest of them.

Fléchelle: I agree with you if the rest of them are men you have no or low interest in. But if your number one man calls and you are not taking the opportunity to be with him and would rather go out with someone you know has low potential for you on principles, then I would have to say that I don't understand you.

Tracy: If one man I do not care much about calls me regularly in advance to schedule a date for every Saturday night, I might just say no in case another better offer presents itself. If I do not get a better offer, then I might just call friends or stay home.

Fléchelle: This is why my "double" and "triple booking" advice is a good way to ensure that you are taking care of yourself. Why would you take the risk of not having a date with a great guy? Unless you are in your late teens or early twenties, believe me, the more time you are losing, the harder it is to find someone who wants to be with you. And besides, I cannot tell you how many times I have seen women have three scheduled dates for a Saturday night and find themselves with no dates at all in the end! Haven't you ever been canceled at the last minute?

I appreciate you sharing your thoughts with me and challenging my "double booking" advice. The reason I am taking this time to write to you is not to make you change your mind. If you are happy with the results you have been getting so far with the way you have been doing things, by all means don't change a thing. But I also know that you want to be married and start a family and that you do not have too much time to lose. If I can help you maximize your chances to get what you want, great! I am only here to help you see the dating world with wide open eyes. Let me know what your thoughts are on this, will you?

Tracy is now happily married.

When you are multiple dating, you have more chances to be double and triple booked on Saturday nights than any other nights.

Ladies, when a man, any man, asks you out on a Saturday night, even if you do not care much for him (for now), say "yes." If you say "no," he will think that you do not care much for him, (which would be correct for now), but he might turn out to be the best man you will ever get to be with in the end. He might just be adequate at the moment, but what if after a few more dates, he turns out to be the best man you have in all your suitors and you have set the precedent that you are not interested in him? Why would you take that risk? When a man asks you out on Saturday night, what is your answer? "YES!" I can assure you that it is better to cancel them at the last minute with the "girlfriend" excuse, than to tell them no, which they rightly translate to: "I am too busy for you!" So please, don't do that.

You will be much softer and have more diplomacy with men when you take care of yourself first by adopting the "double booking" method. When a man who has canceled your date calls you back—and he probably will since you did not blast him when he called you to cancel your date—you will be able to stay light and breezy because that night you were out having the time of your life with another one of your suitors.

My "double booking" advice will help you keep smiling through being canceled, and even stood up. Moreover, it will make you available and visible for your future husband to find you!

I promise, on my honor, to say "yes" to as many men who will ask me out, no matter how many date "promises" I have from others. So help me God.

· · ·

9

What Is The Meaning of Engagement?

Love does not consist in gazing at each other but in looking outword together in the same direction.

Antoine de Saint-Exupery

WHAT IS AN ENGAGEMENT? WHAT PURPOSE DOES IT SERVE? An engagement is a mutual promise to investigate the compatibilities of the couple and move forward to a married life. What is a promise? A promise gives ground to expect a certain outcome.

When a man contracts with a woman into a monogamous relationship leading to marriage and gives her a ring for her to wear publicly, he seriously commits himself to her and to their relationship. A man gives a woman a ring as a symbol of his intentions towards her, and she wears it as a symbol of her commitments towards him and their relationship. Along with that comes a willingness to make known to each family member, friends and the world their love for one another and their intentions to investigate a lifelong commitment to each other.

The engagement came to life in the early 1200s. At that time, engagements were publicly announced to let the community know that a man and a woman would exclusively get to know each other with the intention to find out if they had grounds for an enduring marriage.

If both agreed to move their relationship forward towards marriage, they would then be pledged to each other through the act of betrothal, which is a mutual promise or contract for a future marriage, and a wedding date would be announced. A written and publicly published betrothal added vibrancy and intensified the commitment to one another. It is at that moment that their focus changed from the "me" and "you" to the "we" and "us," as both had a common objective. Later on they would be married in front of God and commoners.

In contemporary Western culture, because sex before marriage is condoned, the meaning of engagement, betrothal and marriage has changed. Couples live together and play house before making up their minds if they want to be married to each other or not. In fact, they try out "married life" before even finding out if they have enough commonality to sustain a marriage. Although this sound like a good deal, it has taken men and women to a non-committed and apprehensive way of life. Men and women are no longer looking into ways of making their relationships work; instead they are looking at ways to eliminate each other before they get to give a serious commitment to one another, all the while using each other as surrogate spouses.

Because of the effect of oxytocin bonding, women tend to be naturally married to their mates while he is test driving her to see if she is worthy enough for him to marry her. It creates a lot of confusion and insecurities in women who just want to be loved, cherished and ultimately honored by the men in whom they have invested their lives, hearts and souls.

As nobody is perfect and because women have made "upgrading" to a new woman so easy for men by allowing themselves to be used as free wives, it doesn't take long for men, usually about two to three years, to tell their free wives that their relationships are "not really working for them." Most men will eventually end up feeling guilty for taking so much from a woman while knowing that she would only be a good time girl. Men know from the onset if they will ever marry a woman or not. But hey, who can blame these men for using women this way? Women are the ones who sell themselves short and act as free wives to men who are barely just lovers. If they do not value themselves more than that, why should men?

By requiring a formal engagement, a woman tells a man that she will not allow him to use her as a free wife. She tells him that he needs to make up his mind and decide if he wants to become serious in his intentions towards her. When a woman is young and has a protective father to watch over her, a man has to go through the ritual of asking the father for his permission to court his daughter. As women get older, and most often their fathers are no longer in the picture, or they are fathers who don't think anything of taking from women without honoring them first, women must be very vigilant and have to be their own fathers and ask for guarantees from men before they give themselves to them.

In the last thirty years or so, women have been giving themselves to men free of commitment in the hope to have a man do right by them and honor them with marriage. This backward way of getting what they want has only taken them down the back road to disappointment and unhappiness. If a woman wants to be married and co-create a family with a husband, she must first find a man who is on the same path as she is and not allow him to use her in any way until he has given her what she needs and wants. No wonder women are feeling empty after giving themselves repeatedly to men who keep on leaving them to marry virtuous women who have told them no to sex before commitment. Of course, we all know a couple or two who had sex on their first date and eventually got married. However, this happened most often after years of her coercing him into marriage and sooner or later, by her giving him an ultimatum in order for him to finally honor her. Why take that risk? Who needs that when you are already in your thirties and ready for a serious commitment?

An engagement is an agreement between a couple to enter into marriage at some future time and most often is accompanied by a formal or informal announcement to friends and families and to the public at large with an announcement in their local newspaper. With this agreement, the couple is known to be "engaged to be married," or just "engaged." The act of engagement is performed in order to negotiate the possibilities of a married life between a man and a woman. The couple will then discuss money, children, friends, time spent together and apart, daily domestic chore responsibilities and the morals and values that will be the foundation that will support their union. This is what an engagement is all about. It is a man and a woman who spend time together in order to find out if they are a good enough match on all the above-mentioned life issues to move forward into a married relationship. This formal pledge does not oblige one party to marry the other. Engagement is not legally binding.

Marriage is a business, and romance has little bearing on the success of a marriage. Because marriage has been romanticized instead of being handled for the financial and social status agreement that it actually is, both men and women are disappointed when their marriage is not all the love and special attentions they thought it would be. Marriage is a contract that should not be taken lightly.

The meaning of engagement nowadays is seen as a public announcement that a couple has decided to marry and has selected a wedding date instead of as an investment into investigating a future together. This contemporary way of life has made men and women enter into sexual relationships without first negotiating their future together, and more than one knee has been scratched this way.

Ladies, if you want to be married, start seeing engagement for what it is: a commitment to look into a married life together, not the culmination of a love affair. Do not be afraid to ask that level of commitment from a man. Getting engaged with a man who is serious enough to not only love you, but honor you as well by giving you the status you deserve, will elevate your relationship to a higher level, which you cannot even start fantasizing about. I can promise you that if you are keeping your commitments to yourself, you will find a man who will respect and honor you enough to give you the commitments you need from him. And once you have had this level of commitment from a man, you will never want to revert to giving yourself to a man with only the hope that he will come through for you.

If a man tells you that he is not ready to commit to engagement because he is not one hundred percent sure that he wants to marry you, then explain to him what an engagement means to you. Chances are he doesn't know what an engagement really means any more than you did before you read this. He will have to ponder about this for a while, but if he is worthy of you, he will come through. If he goes away, thank your lucky stars, because his rejection is your protection.

PART THREE

NEGOTIATING AND RELATING

· · ·

10

When To Give Exclusivity ~ The Talk

Fortune and love befriend the bold.

Ovid

I SUGGEST THAT YOU GET AN ENGAGEMENT RING and a formal commitment before you give sex and exclusivity to a man. I can hear the screams and the outrage already. What do you mean no sex prior engagement? You are crazy! No men will ever give a woman a ring without at least having had sex with her! Even less if you haven't kissed him before! And me! What about me! I want sex, I need sex, I cannot live without sex! I am outraged; who does she thinks she is! She must think she is the best thing since sliced bread if she thinks she can get a ring without giving out sex!

Yes, as a matter of fact I do, and so should you!

Slow down pony, nobody dies from not having sex. People die from not having love, but not from lacking sex. Would you not prefer to make love in the safety of a loving relationship with a man who really loves you instead of being a man's flavor of the month? With a ring and a serious commitment, you will feel honored and cherished from the beginning. There won't be any pulling and wondering.

Remember, this program is for women who are really tired of having been tried on for size over and over and still have yet to be married. This program is for women who may never have had a man propose to her or even offer her a ring, and the only time they heard the word "ring" coming out from a man's mouth is when he got up from her bed and told her, "I'll give you a ring" as he buckled up his pants.

You might not believe that by giving sex to a man for free without a commitment, you are impeding your chances to get married anytime soon. You might think that I simply do not know what I am talking about and that I know nothing about relationships. If so, I would suggest you not to waste your time here and keep doing what you have been doing in the past. There will always be time for you to come back to this program, perhaps in a few years when you feel that you have tried everything else and your eggs are starting to shrivel.

This program is to encourage women to wait before being sexually responsive to a man until he has given her a serious commitment and has invested in a ring for her. A man who invests in a ring is investing himself in the relationship and is a serious man. Think of it: Why would you invest yourself, your heart, and your body in a man who doesn't think that you are good enough for him to commit to? A man has all the rights in the world to take all the time he needs, but really ladies, while he makes up his mind, why should you be on the shelf and miss opportunities to meet men who are ready to be married.

Men know what they want. Do not under estimate them. A man literally will get up one morning and decide that is it now time for him to settle down. Then he'll go out looking for a wife. He very often will marry the next woman he meets. He meets a woman and thinks, "She is nice, good looking enough, has a good mental disposition, doesn't sleep around, and seems as if she would be a good wife," and that's it! It is not more complicated than that. Men are simple. A man wants a good wife who won't sleep with his best friend when he is out of town. Therefore a virtuous woman becomes a valuable commodity. Men appreciate that a woman is not sleeping with *any* men (including them, as men think that women do with other men the same thing they do with them) until she gets a ring. They see her as being virtuous. You do not believe me? Ask around. Ask men what they think about this. Unless they are working you over in order to get you to have sex with them for free, men will tell you that they are ultimately looking for virtue.

You simply must not fall for him before he does for you. Remember, men love to chase and love to have the feeling they had to work for something. You are a prize with a price! And men love a woman who values herself.

Take care of yourself, and the universe will take care of you. By giving a ring, a man really commits himself. Believe me, if a man is not ready, there is no ring that will come from him. And if he is not ready to give you a ring, he certainly is not ready to commit to marriage either. How many years can you afford to waste?

I suggest that before you invest your heart and your soul in a relationship, it would be safer for you to wait for the man to invest himself and his heart first. If he can't take the risk, why should you?

Know that if you are having sex with a man, you are committed to him (remember the oxytocin effects?), and unless he has put a ring on your finger, he is *not* committed to you. Words are cheap. Besides, how can you work towards being in a married relationship if you are with a man who is not ready to bite the bullet and get engaged to you in order to start serious negotiations? Why would a woman work on a relationship and make compromises with a man who is not even sure where this relationship is going? Would it not make you feel insecure to play wife to a man who cannot decide if he is ready to move forward with being in a married relationship with you or not? Would that not make you feel a tad off balance?

Another thing you need to be aware of is that even if a man tells you he wants to be married and have children, and he wants to give all his love to one woman, it doesn't mean *you* unless he asks *you* to marry him. Most women will see such a man as a real good potential and will start giving herself to a man who tells her all these things. Again, words are cheap. Words are so cheap, in fact, that there are married men who tell women they are divorced, even though they are still married to their wives. These men tell women they want to marry them, that they will go shopping for a ring next week, and they can now feel safe to have sex with them! Sure… You're looking for a married man, but married to *you*.

Of course, you can give exclusivity to a man with a verbal commitment to work towards a married relationship, and you might very well get married. It is, however, more risky than waiting to get engaged before you give exclusivity. Since I know that it always comes down that eventually the woman will need to move forward in the relationship, and the man will have to commit with an engagement ring, I find it preferable for women to become exclusive only when a man is ready to make that type of commitment in his life. Remember, if you do not require a formal engagement today in order to give exclusivity and all the goodies that comes with it to a man, you will still have to require it in the future. As the saying goes; "Why buy the cow when the milk is free." I know that some books tell women just to give men their time and themselves for free and hope for the best, but I am not such a gambler.

Do not be afraid to ask for a ring and a formal engagement. If the man doesn't give it to you and goes away, it is for your benefit. Only the right one will stay and love and cherish you the way you deserve to be.

Ladies, please know that we women set the standards in our relationships. Women are the spiritual centers of the family, and men are as good as their women require them to be. So set your standard high, and higher situations will occur in your life. We create our reality by the choices we make. Nobody said it would be easy, but what is the alternative? I don't think that if you keep doing what has not worked in the past, you will have much of a different outcome now. What do you think?

*I promise, on my honor, that I will keep the commitments
I made to myself before I give my sex to a man.
So help me God.*

THE TALK

But how will I tell this to a man? How will I phrase what it is I need and want before moving to the next level with him? Can I do this without stuttering? Is this what I want?

Well you know that you want to be married, and you know that what you have done in the past hasn't work for you, right? Then let me give you the tools you will need in order to get what you need and want from a man. We will call it "The Talk."

"The Talk" is what you will practice while you are out dating multiple men. It will be very easy for you to have the chance to practice "The Talk" since most men will ask you to have sex with them between the first and the third date. Exciting, isn't it? So, let's say that you are out with Joe, this is date number two, and he is holding your hand as he walks you to your car. He pulls your body a little closer to his, sheepishly smiles at you, and asks if he can give you a kiss. You say, "Yes, of course," and present your left cheek. He kisses it, and then says something like, "Well I meant a real kiss… Can I give you a real kiss?" And you say, "What do you mean?" He says, "A kiss on the lips?" "Ahhh…" you say, "I see… Well thank you so much for offering to kiss me. I am glad to see that you feel this way towards me because I sure feel this way towards you too; however, I do not feel comfortable with casual kissing." Then you shut up. Let him recover and get that "deer caught in the headlight" look off his face. He might not recover from it for quite a while, so he might just say, "Oh, okay" and give you his farewell. Or he might ask you what you mean. That is when you have "The Talk."

"The Talk" is when you tell a man what you need from him in order for him to be more than just a date for you. "The Talk" is about what you will need to get in order for the two of you to relate.

Following are a few examples of "The Talk."

SCENARIO ONE:

You: "Well, Joe, as you know, I am looking to be married, and I have decided that I will not become intimate with a man until I am formally engaged with an engagement ring."

Joe: "Wow! Isn't it a bit extreme? I am only asking you for a kiss on the lips, I am not asking you to marry me!"

You: "Yes, I know that in this day and age it sounds extreme. However, I have decided to be intimate only with a man who is serious enough to put an engagement ring on my finger and show the world, his family and friends that I am the woman of his life. I hope you understand my feelings."

Joe: "So that means you are not going to have sex until engaged either?"

You: "Yes, that's right."

Joe: "There is no way in the world I could wait that long in order to have sex with a woman! This is ridiculous."

You: "You have the right to think this way; however, I know that if I would be intimate with you in any way, I would fall so hard for you. You are nice, intelligent and good looking too, and I would just love to feel all the excitement intimacy with you would bring me. However I would feel horrible knowing we would not have discussed the possibility of a relationship first and that we would not be exclusive. It would kill me to know you are out with other women when we're not together. I hope you understand my feelings." Do not try to convince him, you'll never be able to do that. A man has to convince himself to do anything he wants to do. What you want has very little to do with his decision.

Joe: "Well I can't discuss a relationship with you so soon..."

You: "I understand Joe. Well thank you so much for a most beautiful evening. I truly enjoy your company. Good night." Get in your car, and leave. Do not say more than that. He has more to think about than he has had in a long time, if ever.

SCENARIO TWO:

You: "Well, Joe, as you know, I am looking to be married, and I have decided that I will not become intimate with a man until I am formally engaged with an engagement ring."

Joe: "Wow! This sounds great. So is a kiss out of the question?

You: (smiling) "On the lips yes. I find kissing on the lips very intimate, and I know that if I would be intimate with you in any way, I would fall so hard for you. You are nice, intelligent and good looking too, and I would just love to feel all the excitement intimacy with you would bring me. However, I would feel horrible knowing we would not have discussed the possibility of a relationship first and that we would not be exclusive. It would kill me to know you are out with other women when we're not together. I hope you understand my feelings."

Joe: "Of course, I understand. I don't want for you to be hurt. And I don't mind waiting for as long as you will need me to. I really like you a lot. I know this is only our second date, but I care about you, and I am also looking to be married. I like the way you think. Well, can I kiss your cheek and give you a hug?"

You: "Of course." Appreciate the kiss and the hug, and say good night.

Some men might ask you for exclusivity before they ask to kiss you or have sex with you. When that happens, thank him, and tell him that you would love to investigate a serious relationship with him, and tell him what you need in order to take that step with a man. Tell him that you do not take a man seriously until he is serious enough to put an engagement ring on your finger and show the world, his family and friends that you are his woman. Of course, you may want to discuss the type of commitment you will both honor—sexual and social monogamy, longevity, and continuity in a relationship leading to marriage.[1] Let him digest that. If the man is serious, it will make him appreciate you even more, and he will respect your commitments to yourself.

Men who are marriage minded will hear your words as if music to their ears. Men who are not marriage minded will panic at the idea that they would have to do more than buy dinner for a woman in order to get her in the sack. It is all relative. The reason

1 Dr. Pat Allen

I say not to argue your point with a man is that it will not serve you well. You are not out there dating trying to sell yourself to everybody. You are out there being receptive to marriage minded men because your goal is to be married with a man who wants to (a) be married, and (b) be married to *you*. We do not find a good man, a good man finds us. Does this make sense to you? A man who will love you will want to honor you with a ring and an engagement in order to make you feel good and comfortable, knowing that you are being included in his life.

Some men might just come on to you and start grabbing you. These men are not bad, they just need to be told by you how you want them to treat you. Too often, women have chastised men for being gentlemen. Many men think they need to act like a stallion in order to be liked by women. Again, just remember that good masculine men just want to make you happy.

So your date is the passionate, vigorous type? It *is* a good thing that he is trying to get into your pants. Make sure to thank him when he does, by saying something like, "Oh you Big Tiger Man (giggling)! I so much appreciate that you are attracted to me this way, because I sure am attracted to you. However, I have made a commitment to myself that I would keep from being intimate with a man until he would be serious enough to put a ring on my finger and tell his family and friends that I am the woman of his life. If you were as serious as that about me, I would get engaged to you this minute... (pause) What do you think?" Then shut up, and let him think about it.

Practice this as often as you can in front of a mirror first, so that you will feel more comfortable when it is time to come out from your mouth; with practice, you will sound and feel more convinced of your commitment to yourself. He will most probably try again and again; it is his job to try to make you fall to see if you are as good as you say you are. Stay virtuous. Just remember to thank him every time he offers sex to you, and KEEP SAYING the SAME THING every time he asks: "Oh you Big Tiger Man (giggling)! I so much appreciate that you are attracted to me, because I sure am attracted to you. However, I have made a commitment to myself..."

Multiple dating will give you the opportunity to practice having "The Talk." You can have "The Talk" with all the men you go out with. Even if you think he is too short (too fat, too bald) for you, have "The Talk" with him anyway. From the time that you will have "The Talk" with a man to the time you will get a ring from him, you should have enough time to learn more about him and see if this man has the potential to make a good husband to you, and a good father to your children. The short one you did not care much about when you first met him might turn out to be your future husband, if he acts in ways that will allow you to develop respect for him and feel loving feelings towards him.

If you should have a man give you a ring the next time he sees you, I suggest you take it and give him exclusivity. You do not have to have sex with him just because he gives you a ring. A ring is a symbol of his intentions towards you. So please, do not tell a man that "it is too soon to be engaged." Instead, thank him for sharing his intentions with you. You may tell him that you really like him and that you would be ready to start an exclusive relationship with him; however, you are not ready to be sexually intimate just yet; you would let him court you exclusively, and you would be in all aspects his fiancée. A man who is serious enough to become engaged, with a ring, will understand and will wait for you. Of course, if the man expects to have sex that same night and insists on it, and you are not ready, then give him back his ring, and tell him that you are not ready to have sex yet, and he can ask you again further down the line. Keep on dating him and others if he keeps calling you for dates. I would not hold my breath for this one though, I have seen men giving "appeasement rings" to women just to have sex with them.

You might wonder why I suggest for you to accept a ring and give exclusivity to a man that you are not so sure you will ever want to marry, right? The reason is that a good man is very hard to find, and one who is serious enough to give you a ring and wait for you to be ready in order to have sex with you is a man you should *sincerely* consider as a serious contender. The risk of losing the other contenders for this serious one is a calculated risk I suggest you take. Besides, you might tell your other suitors that you are very busy and will be for a couple of weeks. After six to eight weeks of serious negotiations with your new fiancé, you will know for sure if he is someone you will risk losing others for or not.

You have to be discerning, and with practice you will be. My program is very simple—simplistic, in fact. You just withhold what men want the most in order to get what you need first, in your case, a husband. No games involved. The marriage minded man will hear your words as music to his ears and find you even more attractive and precious. The non-marriage minded man will simply go away. This is why you are waiting for the ring. It weeds out the non-serious contenders.

Let's look at two stories: Eve and Melanie. See what lesson you get from both.

· · ·

Dear Fléchelle,

I have been dating a man for the last two months. Clark is absolutely wonderful. We spend a lot of time together at his place since he has a little boy who is as adorable as could be. Clark knows that I will not be exclusive with anyone until a man has formally taken me off the market with an engagement and a ring.

Clark tells me that he loves me and that he cannot see life without me anymore. We even went looking at engagement rings together. Now Clark is telling me that he needs to be more certain that I am the one for him, but cannot concentrate on this as long as I am available to others. He wants for me to give him exclusivity without a ring.

I do not know what to do. Clark is a good man, and I don't want to lose the opportunity of a life with him in the hope that I will meet someone else out there. I am thirty-six years old and want children. Please help. Eve

Dear Eve,

How long are you ready to give this man exclusivity? Six months, a year, two years? If you were in you late twenties or very early thirties, I would support your giving him exclusivity without sex until you receive a ring in six months to a year. However, at thirty-six, you do not have much time to waste if you want to start your family.

This is the way I see it. Let's say you own a car dealership, and a customer comes to see you and tells you that he is extremely interested in buying one of your cars and that he cannot really see his life without it. He wants to negotiate a purchase deal. You sit down with him, go over all the features, let him test drive it, and then tell him the price. He tells you that without any doubt he will buy this car, as he wants it so much. But just to make sure, he would like to drive the car for six months or so, and if after six months, he still hasn't made up his mind completely, then he will return the car, and he believes you would not be any poorer for it. What would you think of that? Or let's say that you have a client who wants to hire your services as a computer programmer, but he is not really sure if he will need the program when you are done. So would you do the work for free, he asks? Well, you will tell him that you are a qualified programmer and won't risk losing a paying client while spending your valuable time working for him for free, right? What do you think? If you would think that it would be a good deal for you to work for this client for free, then I would need to ask you "Where's your brain? Would it be on oxytocin by any chance?"

While giving him exclusivity sounds good to you right now because you are probably bonded to him through oxytocin as you have been playing house with him, keep in mind that you would be putting your product on hold in the hope that this particular client would eventually buy it. Do you think that this would be a sound business decision? It seems quite risky to me. Can you sacrifice your chance of marriage and children for this man who has little vision about your future? The time you are waiting while the eggs get old is the sacrifice you are making. Clark knows your price and does not want to pay it. He wants you for free. He has a right to want you for free without having to commit to you, but you have the right to say yes or no. Are you going to keep your commitment to yourself, or are you going to go for the lesson? He is testing you to see how well you value yourself. If you do not value yourself, why should he value you? Good luck in making your decision. Your future depends on it.

· · ·

Here's a letter from Melanie who thinks that she might lose her guy if she doesn't put out:

Dear Fléchelle,
I need your help, as I don't know what to do in these circumstances. I am dating a masculine gentleman. Usually, I am very feminine and receptive towards men, allowing the men to lead, but with this one I found myself inviting him to a couple of functions and parties. Should I let him do all the inviting since he is the masculine leader type of man? Also I feel I will lose him if I don't have sex with him as he will think that I am too demanding by requesting a serious commitment before having sex. He hasn't called me in over a week. I don't know what to do. Melanie

Dear Melanie,
A) Wait for his phone call.

B) When he calls, be responsive; return his calls as you would any girlfriend's.

C) Inviting a man you date to a party or function is not masculine, it is nice. Men like to be invited to special outings where they would enjoy your company.

D) And last but not least, I can guarantee you that if you have sex with him with ANYTHING LESS than the commitment you have asked of him, you WILL lose him, as he will lose respect for you for not keeping your commitments to yourself.

Keep those commitments you have made to yourself. A good man won't leave you because you do not give him sex. Men do not marry women for the sex they give. Men marry women who respect them and respect themselves. All you have to do is be appreciative and respectful. Be yourself and have fun with your dates. And most importantly, you must not be afraid to lose a man in order to catch a man. Good luck.

· · ·

11

How Friendly Should I Be Without Having Sex Until Engaged?

Men don't marry vaginas, they marry virtue!

Dr. Pat Allen

BE FRIENDLY! WHY WOULDN'T YOU BE? Just don't have penetrative sex with men until you get what you've decided you would settle for. If you think you can handle the kissing and hugging type of sex without having penetration, then do it. It is more risky, but you need to judge for yourself what works and doesn't work for you.

Men love to be called sweet names: Tiger, Sweetheart, Sweetie, Darling, Love, Big Man, whatever you feel like calling them. It makes a man feel special. Think "Southern Belle." Besides, when you multiple date, it's easier to call them generic names such as Darling, so that you don't call Rob by the name of Steve, or vice versa. So Darling they all are, and darlings they are.

You can call men any names you like, even "Love," as long as you keep your head clear from false dreams that he is your knight in shining armor, the one and only, coming to save you. At least not until you get the commitment you want from him.

I suggest keeping the couch visits to the extreme minimum. Couches have a way of making people feel comfortable and more intimate. If you want to sit on a couch, go to the lobby of a large hotel where there are always nice big comfy couches where you can feel intimate with your date without getting too intimate. This way, you'll be in public, and this should decrease his fervor (and yours) as a chaperon would. If you are looking for a fun thing to do on a rainy Saturday afternoon after your lunch date, bring a social board game such as Scrabble or Backgammon to your local public library, and enjoy a fun afternoon with less sexual tension than you would have watching a movie at home sitting on the couch!

So keep it in public, and please do not invite him for a nightcap unless you feel very strongly you could resist him. I know few women who could, and why would you want to jeopardize your position? Do not invite him over unless there is someone in the house, okay? Play it safe. He will appreciate you for being the woman you are, and, as you know, men think that you are doing the same thing with all your dates that you are doing with him. The more highly the marriage minded man will think of you, the less he will want to see you trip and fall, because if you did, he would need to make a decision about you, and that might not include the word marriage in it. He wants a virtuous woman. So be vigilant, and do not put yourself in situations that might not show you at your best.

Men know that they are privileged to be in your presence and appreciate the chance to court you. Therefore, know that you are the one guarding the gate. Marriage-minded men will wait for you to decide when, where, and how far they can go with you. Treat men with respect and appreciation, and they'll hang around.

Some women think that men want to have wives who are horny all the time, when in fact, men are looking for wives they can relax with, and in the eventuality that they would be unable to perform for a while, know that their wives are not going to be looking for other partners to satisfy them. Men need to know that their wives are virtuous women who can be without sex and will be waiting for them.

Another thing, please stay away from the magazines that have all the answers on how to please a man in bed. I picked up a copy of one of these magazines at the beauty shop recently and was shocked by an article telling women what to do in bed in order to keep their men. It was almost soft porn in its description. I could not believe what I was reading. Now, I am no prude, and I am all for education to develop physical skills, but really, who are these people telling women they should give themselves sexually to men in order not to lose them? So please, stay away from these magazines; it will only mess up your head. Besides, busy masculine men do not read these magazines, so they won't know this is what some magazines tell women they should do to them. Unless you know a man really well anyway, why would you want to seduce him in bed? Let him seduce you. If you seduce a man the way some magazine tells you, he'll probably think that you have been with lots of men since you have so much experience when, in fact, you've never maneuvered this way with any man before but only read about the technique.

Many men complain about not being able to seduce a woman anymore because women always beat them to the punch. It is not surprising to hear this when women practice what they read in these magazines; being aggressive is what they are taught! Ladies, believe me when I tell you that men do not marry for sex. Men are simple; you do not have to hang from the chandelier to please a man. Be nice and appreciative; men will love you for that. So please, do not jump on a man, any man. Let him court and seduce you. It might be a new experience for you, and you might need patience, as marriage minded men wouldn't want to rush you into bed with them. And as you know, patience is a virtue, so make it work for you.

So how friendly should you be? Hugging, hand holding, little kisses are all fine things you can do with a man who shows you, by his actions, that he is a valuable suitor. You will find that you can melt a man's heart more quickly with a smile and a sexy gaze while he is holding your hand and telling you about his life's dreams than you can by making him scream in bed. Be friendly enough for him to know that you are interested in him, but reserved enough to dissuade physical intimacy before engagement.

It is really hard out there in the dating world to say no to sex before engagement, as the competition is really stiff. Again, this program is not for the faint at heart. Because women do not value their sexuality and give their sex, commitment free, after only one or two dates, men have gotten used to not valuing women and expect having free sex after wining and dining a woman a couple of times. Many men simply take women out for coffee dates a couple of times, and they know they can have an easy roll in the hay. Women give commitment-free sex to a man thinking he will fall in love with her if she gives it to him. Wrong!

It used to be that men needed to marry us in order to have sex with us. Nowadays men expect to have free-of-commitment sex almost on demand. Women have been so giving that they have spoiled men. The result is, men might not call you back upon learning that you will not have sex with them prior to engagement as they might think there is something wrong with you. Do not feel discouraged about that. If a man rejects you for this, know that it is simply in your favor. However, it will not deter a marriage minded man; instead he will be challenged by that. He will try to make you trip just to see if you are as good as you say you are; it is his job to do so, but he won't go away for that reason. For lack of respect, marriage minded men will leave you, but not for lack of sex.

Even a good man might go away upon hearing of your "no sex before engagement" commitment you've made to yourself. Remember, men have been spoiled and will think they *deserve* sex with you without having to commit. Hasn't this always been the way? Women fell for them on demand and never asked for anything in return. Do not worry, you might be a novelty for him, but if he is a good man and a serious man, he will think about what you have to offer and decide for himself if you are enough of a good thing for him to have to commit to before having sex.

Of course, because you will be taking care of yourself by multiple dating, having some men fall by the wayside will not deter you from keeping your commitments, continuing to date, and meeting potential husbands, right? After all, until you have a ring on your finger, you are a single woman going on about your life.

The more you'll practice your dating skills, the better you'll get, and soon enough all this will just be as natural to you as eating and breathing. And I can guarantee you that you will be in demand more than ever.

· · ·

Dear Fléchelle,
I am on your "No Kissing Plan," and it works really well for me. I never have had so many men being interested in me. They all know that I am not kissing anyone until engaged, and each is doing more for me than any previous men I have ever dated. I want to be a little more touchy feely without sending the wrong signal. How can I let them know that it would be okay to be more playful, without giving them the impression that it will end up in the bedroom. I want them to know that I am interested. Tanya

Dear Tanya,
You can be friendly with a man in a romantic way, instead of in a sexual way. You can hold hands, let him kiss your cheeks, and gently stroke his arm while sitting at the theater, for example. You can give him a big kiss on the cheek and a big hug at the end of the date and thank him for the most wonderful time he has provided you. Men know that a woman is interested in them by the amount of genuine attention she gives them when around them, not by the amount of sex she gives them. I am glad that you are the recipient of these men's attentions and generosity. A woman gets much more by being sweet with the men she dates and by acting feminine and lovely than she would by giving away her body and soul trying to satisfy their immediate and short lived sexual appetites. Keep up the good work.

· · ·

12

If You Should Fall

*Right actions in the future are the best
apologies for bad actions in the past.*

Tryon Edwards

MEN CAN BE VERY IRRESISTIBLE, CAN'T THEY? I know… I love men too. They can be charming, intelligent, kind, funny, handsome, very handsome, generous, caring and loving, with many more beautiful attributes than I can mention here. So if you should fall, don't worry, you can always get up again, hopefully with as tiny a knee scratch as possible.

Let's say you have been seeing Romeo for a few weeks and he is "the man" of your dreams. Romeo is a "Romeo." He is fun, charming, gorgeous, with a dimple on his left cheek, and sparkling eyes when he looks into yours. He is what I call "The Package."

Romeo has taken you out, told you all the good things you want to hear; he wants marriage, children, wants to take you to Italy to meet his family, tells you Mama will adore you, talks to you about the little Romeos you'll have together, and how you will live happily ever after… You know what I mean?

It started with little kisses and deep hugs. Then the kisses became passionate and the hugs deeper. Then… Well, of course, I would not have been able to resist either.

You find yourself being in a sexual relationship with Romeo (he is fantastic in bed too), and you ask yourself, "What happened?" You were so dedicated to finding a husband, not just another lover. And Romeo doesn't talk about Italy anymore, even worse, he tells you that his uncle in Italy is sick, and that he will have to go "alone," because his uncle is the pillar of the family, it would be disrespectful to bring you and your happiness to Italy, since the poor man is so sick...

And last night, he was supposed to call you around seven o'clock to tell you what time he would pick you up for dinner, and ended up calling you at ten, apologizing and telling you that his boss called him in his office, and he could not get away, not even for a phone call. But if it would be okay, he could come to see you and sleep at your place overnight. Do you still have any of that delicious spaghetti you cooked for him last night?

You have called all your girlfriends to ask them what they think. Your single girlfriends are sympathetic but they have no advice for you. Your married girlfriends are ruthless. They want to know what's wrong with you, why you can't just find a good man and settle down.

You talked to him before about where your relationship is going, but he is so busy and always has to rush out the door.

It is time to take the bull by the horns and take action.

There are only a few things you can do at this point. You can either stay in the relationship for as long as you can in the hope that Romeo will see the light and see what a perfect wife you would be and hope you won't lose three years or more of your life in this relationship, or whatever this is, or you can backtrack to the commitments you made to yourself.

I know that you do not want to lose another three years of your life. But I also know that you are oxytocin bonded at this point, and that under it's influence, it is extremely difficult to make a sound decision about your life. Now it is time for you to be ruthless about setting aside the bonding you feel. Easier said than done, but imperative. It will hurt. It will hurt like hell. You can do it.

When Romeo next calls, you must tell him that you have to talk to him about your relationship, and ask him if now would be a good time for him to hear you out. If he says that he cannot talk right now, ask him when would be a good time to talk, and set an appointment with him. He might call you again, or he might not, knowing very well what you want to talk to him about. Romeo is not stupid, you gave him "The Talk" on your third date. He knows what you want and need, and besides, he senses that you are not feeling very comfortable these days.

If he does keep your appointment, you must tell him that although you love him very much, and you think he is a wonderful man, you made a mistake in becoming sexually involved with him without having the commitment you need. Tell him that you feel uncomfortable and unsafe, and that unless the two of you are engaged, you will not sleep with him anymore, and will resume dating others until you are engaged with a ring on your finger. He might just say: "Of course, Honey, I understand. What is it that you need? Do you want for us to get engaged? No problem." Great, schedule with him a visit to the jeweler, get engaged, and move on with your relationship. If he says: "Honey, I understand, but you see, so many things are going on right now, my uncle is sick, and my Mama could not handle the news of our engagement; it would kill her that her little Romeo would be leaving her…" Thank him for the time you have spent together and thank your lucky stars that you haven't lost more years of your life with this Romeo!

Give him eight weeks (Dr. Allen says that it can take up to eight weeks for a man's brain to figure out if he loves you or not, and what he wants to do about it, and so on), as he might come around and step up to the plate. Mark your calendar. He may come back to you on that last day of the eight weeks! Do not sleep with anyone else (hopefully until you get engaged with a ring) for at least eight weeks, so if he comes back, you will be open to hear him out, as you will not be bonded with someone else. However, if another man offers you a ring with the commitment you need within that period of time, take it. A bird in the hand… Besides, you do not need to have sex with this new potential husband until the eight weeks are over, or until you are ready and want to.

Get your commitment list out. Read it. Read it again, and again, and again. Romeo was a lesson for you. You will not fall for another man anytime soon. You have made a commitment to yourself, and you will keep it. "What doesn't kill us makes us stronger" is one of my favorite mantras. Post your personal ad, blow your nose, put on your uniform, and go back out there. Don't settle for less than what you want. Appreciate what men give you, but protect your heart by keeping the commitments you have made to yourself. You need to keep your heart and your sanity intact while going through the tribulations of dating, so that you can be found by the right husband for you. Do not invest your heart in a man who has not *first invested himself* in you. Keep the faith. Your husband is around the corner.

．　　．　　．

Here's a letter from Robin, who feels she might have sold herself short:

Dear Fléchelle,
Three months ago I decided to give exclusivity to Richard, one of the men I was dating. I wanted to wait until we were engaged to give him exclusivity, but Richard convinced me that the best way to proceed was for us to be in an exclusive sexual monogamous relationship. So we did.

I just don't feel that he treats me fairly; he calls me at the last minute and only to hang out at his place. He does not take me out to dinner or on dancing dates anymore. I miss the man he used to be. He hasn't called me for a week and a half, and my girlfriend saw him at a bar last night with his friends, and they were all very friendly with the women sitting beside them.

I feel crummy and sick to my stomach. I cannot believe what is happening. I cannot believe he treats me this way. Where did things go wrong? Robin

Dear Robin,

I am sorry you have had to go through this ordeal. When the only commitment we have is one of exclusivity and monogamous sex, that is what we get; a man who is committed to exclusivity and monogamous sex, nothing more. You see, when we wait to have a formal engagement with a man, he will have made public his intentions to "husband" us. "Husband" is a verb, and it means that a man takes care of a woman physically, mentally, emotionally, and in many cases, financially. Therefore, when a man commits himself through the act of giving us a ring and making the engagement public, then the rest falls into place, and this man will call, and will mostly do what is right towards us. When we have only a monogamous sex relationship, that's what we get, monogamy and sex.

Hang on to your commitments to yourself next time, and give exclusivity to a man who is serious enough to put a ring on your finger and tell his family and friends that you are the woman of his life.

Tell Richard that you have thought again about your commitment to him and have decided that you will stop having sex with him. Tell him that you will resume dating him and others, as you are ready to be engaged to a man who will work towards being in a married relationship with you. Good luck to you.

I promise, on my honor, that I will not give myself to a man before he commits to me, loves me, gives to me, cherishes me, and protects me. So help me God.

13

Masculine Energy Gives ~ Feminine Energy Receives

Men fall in love when they give, women fall in love when they receive.

Dr. Pat Allen

ALTHOUGH THE FEMINIST MOVEMENT HAS HELPED women emancipate in the work force, in politics and in social situations, it has also misguided them in some ways. It inadvertently gave women the impression they had to become equal partners (instead of complementary partners) in their relationships with men. That included but was not limited to attaining a career, becoming competitive, and paying their way. As a byproduct of the movement, they became convinced they had to carry their own weight and that being a receptive woman, a stay-at-home mother, or a stay-at-home wife was degrading to their women's egos. Women felt uncomfortable to receive from the opposite sex— everything ranging from love, financial and emotional support, to sperm. Many women these days think nothing of paying for the sperm they need in order to conceive.

Dr. Allen explains very well the synergy between receiving and giving back in great details in her books and seminars. I want to touch on the subject here in order to give you some day-today examples of what happens when a woman gives too much (masculine action), versus receiving (feminine response).

To give you an idea of what nature intended in order for the male and female energy to flow freely between men and women, lets look at what nature had in mind in regards to the laws of giving and receiving as it applies to the nature of men and women.

Men are built to give. Male apparatus was created in order to give. Women are built to receive. Female apparatus was created in order to receive. I am a strong believer that when life situations go amiss, the best way to find the way back is to look at nature itself and how it function.

I remember being at one of Dr. Allen's seminars where she said, "Go to any hardware store and ask for the male component of an electrical outlet, and it will always have prongs. Ask for the female component of an electrical outlet, and it will always have sockets." That's true, I thought, male components always have prongs, and female components always have sockets. Undeniably, nature follows an order. Male penetrates, female receives.

Now let's look at what happens when a woman over-gives to a man instead of being responsive by receiving and giving back.

Rebecca is a modern, smart woman who excels at everything she tries. She can paint, write, cook, and owns a film production company. She has produced quite a few movies and had a couple of kids in between her endeavors. She is very successful in her career and in all aspects of her life except her love life. Men are attracted to her inner and outer beauty and flock around her whenever she goes out to do simple daily activities such as going to the market. Rebecca came to see me because she just did not understand why the men she liked did not stay with her even when the relationship was so promising, and the only ones who hung around always ended up taking from her.

I asked her to tell me about the type of men she attracted, and how she related to them. She said that she liked masculine men who were strong-minded with a gentle soul, men with whom she could feel safe. She liked men who liked to laugh and eat good food. Rebecca, being a great cook, enjoyed serving great meals to men. At first, she said, they would take her out, but she was so much of a homebody that she soon would start inviting them to eat at her house. When they wanted to take her out to a steak house, she would insist on cooking them steaks at home. When they wanted to eat pasta, she would tell them to come over, put their feet up, and she would make them the best pasta they ever had. If they would ask her if she needed for them to bring something, she would say, "Just bring yourself."

After talking to me for a short period of time, I started to recognize the pattern she had with men. Rebecca was a giver. It is very hard for a giving woman to give up that habit. Rebecca was strong and was a woman used to getting things done her way. I told her she needed to stop giving. She did not understand and looked at me as if I was speaking to her in tongues. I told her again she needed to stop giving to men. She stopped talking and looked at me and said, "But isn't giving feminine?" I said, "No, giving is masculine." She looked dumbfounded and told me she did not understand at all how I could say that giving was masculine instead of feminine. She told me it did not make any sense to her.

I could see that she was unable to grasp the concept. I started to talk to her about basic biology. We talked about prongs and sockets, penetrative energy, and receptive energy. Slowly she started to understand how and why nature intended for men to give and women to receive.

I explained to her that every time a man tried to give to her, he tried to penetrate her energy field. And every time she refused his giving, she refused his penetrative masculinity. I am sure it doesn't come to you as a surprise that men like to penetrate, and I am sure it is no surprise to you either that men do not like to be penetrated, right?

When a woman gives to a man, he can only take it for so long before he needs to find the exit door. Men do not have a receiving apparatus. They only have a giving apparatus. Do I need to say more? When women give to men, these men feel the women's attempted penetration, and it simply does not feel good to them. Therefore, men start feeling uncomfortable, and they go away. Any questions? Feminine energy men will stay around because it feels good to them to receive, and they'll keep on taking until you stop giving. Then they'll move on to the next overly generous woman who will give to them and satisfy their feminine nature.

So, please, ladies, next time you want to give to a man or push your ideas and opinions down his throat, can you please keep in mind the view that they have nowhere to put it? Then maybe it will be easier for you to understand why masculine men do not like to be smothered and be told what to do.

When you allow men to penetrate you, you allow yourself to become vulnerable, which is very appealing for the masculine man. Masculine men like to penetrate and feel that the women are like putty in their hands. A vulnerable feminine woman is a woman who needs a masculine protective man. Men like to feel needed. By allowing men to give to you and do for you, you are empowering men to grow to their best potential. By accepting from a man, you are sanctioning a man's growth into his manliness. The more manly empowered your man will be, the more feminine empowerment you will feel. The more feminine you will feel, the best of your potential will grow.

Men need women as much as women need men in order to grow spiritual love. You can love your parents, your family, your friends, but in order to grow spiritual love, you need to have a partner who loves you whom you can love back. Life takes on a new meaning when you have love from a partner as an element in your life. And most certainly, life has more meaning when you have someone to love you, whom you can love back.

In order to balance the energy of give and give back, I gave Rebecca an assignment. She would not give anything more to a man than her presence, her appreciation, and her respect, until the man gave her three times more than she would usually accept. She had to accept three dates in which she was the recipient of a man's generosity before she could give back to him. I suggested she give back by handing him meals from the left over food she had prepared for herself and her family, which she would put in containers for him to take home. She could bake cookies and cakes and prepare care packages of her delicious desserts for him to enjoy when he was away from her. Since she also was an avid reader, I suggested she could cut up articles that would be of interest to him and put it in the bag with the other goodies he would take home with him.

This was a tall order for Rebecca as she did not feel useful unless she was "doing." In having her prepare food "to go" as give backs, which she would prepare when away from men, she was forced to only "be" when she was with men on dates.

With practice she was able to relax and be herself in her relationships with men and feel more confident being herself as a receiving and receptive woman than she had ever felt as a giving, penetrative woman.

Rebecca now lives with her boyfriend on his ranch on the coast of California. She stays conscious of her overly giving nature and takes a step back when she finds her boyfriend feels smothered by her. She has grown into her femininity, which in turn allows her more creativity in her everyday life.

Please, ladies, leave behind your competitive ways in your relationships with men. Do not try to be better men than they are. I am sure that you are very capable of doing everything by yourself, but by doing everything on your own and not enlisting men to do for you or refusing their help, you risk being alone. If you want to be in a relationship with a man, you have to let him do his part, no matter how much it hurts when you see what a better job you would do if you could only do it yourself. Moreover, never tell a man, "Let me show you how to do it..."

Nobody said that you can never give to men. The best way women can give to men is as givebacks. Giving back to a man in proportion to what he gives you balances the energy between the two of you. Practice giving back, instead of giving. Make your giving back an act of returned generosity and a gesture of appreciation instead of penetrative (masculine) generosity. It is really easy to practice, and once you have learned the skill of feminine giving through the action of giving back, you will feel centered and anchored and will have more appreciative men around you who simply will want increasingly to give to you.

.   .   .

Following is Cynthia's letter in which she writes that she is trying to salvage a two-year relationship that is on the path to extinction.

Dear Fléchelle,
Steven and I met three years ago on an Internet dating service. We are both in our late thirties and want to start a family. We love each other very much, but it seems that our idealistic view of life got the best of each other.

I am a masculine energy woman who decided to curb my masculinity in order to live as a feminine woman with a masculine man. Steven fell in love with me because he said I was soft and feminine. We both left our city apartments and purchased an old bed and breakfast inn in a remote corner of New Hampshire. The inn was badly in need of repair, and we decided that we would live on my income and our savings while Steven would oversee the needed renovation work. We had our ups and downs during this transition period. The renovations are now over, and we have vacationers enjoying our lovely inn.

Steven is overdue to return to work but can't seem to make a go of it. He says he can't find any work and is thinking about changing his career for one where he would feel better at expressing himself. I am overworked and worried to death as I have put my life savings into this venture. He says I am worrying for nothing and that I am a nag who pushes him to drink more than he should. I am afraid about our future. Do you have any suggestions for us?
Cynthia

Dear Cynthia,

I am sorry that you find yourself in this predicament. The bad news is that you are either with a feminine energy man, or a masculine energy man who is not as masculine as you are, which makes you the masculine energy in your couple. A strong masculine man would have said "no" to have his feminine energy woman finance their lifestyle. He would not have been able to be penetrated like this by a woman and would have made arrangements both to work and make it possible to fix your place up. And you say that he drinks too much? No wonder, he needs to forget his squashed masculinity, and drinking allows him to live in the right side of his brain, his feminine side. That is why he is thinking about a new career, a career where he would live in the right side of his brain.

Cynthia, right now Steven is rightfully resentful of you for turning out to be a man, and it is important for you to get in touch with what you really want and what you are really able to do. All is not lost if you still love each other.

My suggestion to you is to anchor yourself in your femininity, let the ball drop, and let him pick up the pieces. In doing so, you will allow him to be the man he wanted to be for you when he met you as a feminine energy woman. Somewhere along the line, against your best wishes, you reverted to being the masculine leader, which you know so well how to be. In the life situation you found yourself in, it is very normal that you had this setback. Just put yourself back in the energy you were when you met him. You will start gaining respect for him again, which you seem to have lost along the way. A woman can only love a man she respects, and a man can only love a woman who respects him.

Let him be the masculine energy entity of the relationship. If he picks up the ball and fixes the problems you both have, then you'll be with the man you wanted to be with. If he doesn't, better know right now so that you can cut your losses, move on, and find a masculine energy man that will be strong enough to be with you. Good luck!

· · ·

14

Relinquishing Control

> *The softest things in the world overcome*
> *the hardest things in the world.*
>
> Lao Tzu

WHAT WILL YOU HAVE WHEN YOU STOP BEING the world's chief executive officer? A lot more fun!

One big thing you will gain from letting go of control with men is peace. You will feel more peaceful than ever when you let go of your controlling issues with men. You will feel free. Think of it, all you will have to do is take care of yourself, make sure you are safe, look good, smell good, smile and be graceful with the men you will date. That's all.

By stopping the control of every little thing that happens in your dating life, you will have the chance to sit back and enjoy life while men will be busy making sure that you are having a good time.

Even if you are not happy that he changed your plans at the last minute and invited you to his nephew's third birthday party instead of taking you to that great restaurant where the two of you would have spent a lavish evening, don't mention a thing to him about it. First, you will probably not be able to make him change his mind and keep his previous engagement with you and second, if he accepts to forgo his nephew's birthday party to please you, you will probably live to regret it, if he ever calls you again. Wear a pair of comfortable shoes and clothes you won't mind getting stained if you just happen to sit on a chair where a two-year-old boy just wiped his chocolate covered hands on the seat or if an adorable four-year-old little girl drops her grape juice on your lap. See it as a good occasion to meet his family and find out more about him.

If a man wants to take you to watch a gory movie, which you have absolutely no desire to see, go anyway. Make sure to bring a paper bag if you have a sensitive stomach and plan to spend a lot of time in the bathroom. When the scenes become too much for you to handle and even closing your eyes is not enough, go to the bathroom or wait in the hallway and ask an usher to let you know when the gory scenes are over. Do not try to control him in doing it your way or try to convince him to go and see a movie you would like to see. Don't make him regret asking you out instead of calling his buddy Arnie. He will appreciate your making an effort to please him and will probably take you to a more pleasant movie next time. And if he only likes gory movies and never takes your feelings into consideration, stop seeing him, but do not try to control him.

Trying to control men never works. They might let you do it for a while, but they will eventually grow resentful and will either go passive aggressive on you or will simply go away.

You will find while dating that, unfortunately, some men arrive late on dates—use it in your favor. While waiting for them, smile and flirt with other men around (they might be waiting for their date who are late). When your date finally shows up, you won't be so upset if you have had the chance to give your phone number to a man or two.

Even though it might sound like a good idea to snap at him if he arrives at your house an hour late to pick you up for dinner, don't. Just put a post-it note on your front door saying "I was hungry and left for dinner. Sorry I've missed you." Next time if he is late, he'll call to make sure you'll be waiting for him.

If he keeps taking phone calls when the two of you are out to dinner, don't make faces at him, just take your post-it pad out, write on one of them "I am going to the bathroom," give it to him and leave. When you come back, if he is still on the phone, go back. Keep checking on him, and when he is off the phone, sit down and continue to eat. Of course, do not leave your food if you do not know a man well enough (he may put drugs in it), but after dating him for a while, you should feel comfortable enough to leave your food with him without fearing that he would tamper with it. If you have dated a man for many dates—like five or six—and still do not feel comfortable enough to leave your food, then maybe there is something wrong going on with this man, and you'll have to ask yourself if he is worth the stress.

If a man talks to you about his ex-wife or tells you what his friends think of her or of you, for that matter, don't tell him you don't want to hear about his ex or his friends, just let it go in one ear and out the other. Listen to him only when he has something worthwhile to say. In fact, you should practice this selective hearing as much as you can, as men and women all say things here and there that would have been better left untold. Consider the source when you hear something upsetting, and let it go.

Do not tell a man he needs to dress differently, get a new car, a new haircut, a new place to live, get rid of his dog and his hamster, and ask for a promotion at work. If you do not like the way he dresses, his car, his haircut, his place, his dog and hamster, and think he doesn't make enough money, leave him. Better leave a man for not being good enough for you than trying to control him. Better for you and better for him.

If you do not like his family and/or his friends, you might consider not entering into a relationship with this man. Do not try to turn him against them in your favor. Think of it, he has known his family and his friends for much longer than he has known you, so his leaving them for you is a very improbable outcome. And chances are that if you do not like his family and his friends, you'll probably not like him much either when you really know him. So move on to a better man for you.

Every time you feel words trying to push their way out of your mouth in order to tell a man what to do, why to do it, how to do it, and when to do it, stop yourself immediately. You will do better not to nag and control a man. If he does something you know you could not live with, you can talk to him about it to see if it is something he might be willing and capable to change, or leave him. If you are thinking about voicing your disapproval to a man, just make sure that you are ready to see him walk. Some men do not recover from criticism.

If you have never let a benevolent man lead and control, please consider it. Your new attitude towards men, which will tell them "you're in charge," will soften you and will allow a man to fall in love with you, as he will feel respected and will see you as an agreeable, non-competitive woman who is a complementary partner to his life.

Of course, you are not expected to be only beautiful and unheard for the men you will date, just try not to control them. Nobody likes to be told what to do. You will get more of what you want by letting a man be himself and let him provide for you his way and by your getting along. Try to be as easy-going as possible. When you'll be married with a few kids, you'll be happy to be married to a take-charge type of man who will help you with the many chores and responsibilities of marriage and parenthood. And don't forget, until he puts a ring on your finger, he is only practice.

I promise, on my honor, to let go of my control issues with men. So help me God.

•   •   •

Dear Fléchelle,
I have a problem with control. Even though I know that I am being petty, I hold on and need to always be right. How can I stop doing this? Amy

Dear Amy,
Just stop doing it!

15

A Feminine Woman on a Date

There is a woman at the beginning of all great things.

Alphonse de Lamartine

IT TAKES A VERY STRONG WOMAN to take on the challenge of being vulnerable. Only a woman who is solidly anchored in her femininity can be totally vulnerable and at the same time feel powerful.

When out on a date, let the man pay for you both. Do not take your wallet out and try to outman him by putting your cash on top of his. A woman who is looking for a masculine man, a leader type, will let him take care of her financially his own way on a date.

If you do not like the way he treats you, then do not be with him. Go out and find someone better suited to treat you the way you need and want. DO NOT tell him you would rather go to an expensive French restaurant and offer to pay the difference it would cost him to take you to the more modest one he suggested. That is disrespectful and inappropriate. If you want to eat at an expensive French restaurant rather than a modest one, then find a man who will wine and dine you at such a restaurant or go with a girlfriend.

While we are on the subject of restaurants, I want to address something I hear over and over from women. Some women say they do not want to meet men for dinner and give excuses such as, "If I don't like him, I don't want to be stuck having to spend that much time with him." This is totally ridiculous. How many people do you know that you dislike so much, you could not even have dinner with them? You make it sound like you know many people like that. I personally cannot think of anyone I dislike that much. There are some people I might not care to have dinner with, but still, I could sit for a whole meal with them. My program is for women who enjoy spending time with men and especially are looking for a long-term mate. What does it tell a man about your level of commitment to find a husband if you won't even want to risk having a meal with him? So stop it. I do not want to hear about coffee dates either. Because of women like you, now men are afraid to ask women out for dinner because "they are afraid to impose." Really! I cannot tell you how many men tell me how happy they are when women tell them they don't like coffee dates. These are real men, they are generous, and they want to provide. Please let them, if not for you, at least for the future women they will meet who appreciate a really good man. Enough said.

Men like to please the women they are with—their own way. A man might ask you where you would like to go for dinner. Do not take this as his trying to figure out where he will take you; he usually won't take your advice anyway. He might ask you that just to figure out the amount of money you would cost him "after marrying you." So if you like to dine at expensive restaurants all the time and would not think of having dinner anywhere else, then tell him the names of these restaurants. I think it's best to choose something in the middle. There are many restaurants that serve decent food without costing two hundred dollars for dinner.

Therefore, if a man asks you to pick a restaurant for dinner, have three suggestions already lined up. You can say "Well, I don't know what type of food you like, but there is an Italian restaurant on Pier Avenue that is very good. Down the street from there is a great Japanese restaurant which serves both excellent sushi and cooked Japanese fusion food. There is also a French restaurant on 7th Street that serves some really good country French food." Then shut up and let him decide. Do not be upset if he says, "All these suggestions sound good. Let's go to Mr. Won Ton. I like their egg rolls and chicken cashews…"

If you do not like Chinese food, consider this: you could tell him, "I do not like Chinese food, let's go Italian instead." Or you could say: "I'd prefer French food instead." Or you could say: "Yes. That's sounds great. I have never been there…" The first two answers won't get you very far, believe me. The latter one will make him feel respected for his decision-making and leadership. Even if you cannot stand Chinese food, keep in mind that this is only a date and might be the only time for the rest of your life that you will have to suffer the sight of this food. If you absolutely can't because you are allergic to the "air" in a Chinese restaurant, then decline and start finding your next date, because even if he takes you to a French restaurant, the likelihood of his calling you back is very slim. Men want to marry women who get along.

A feminine woman is easy going. The best words you can use with a man are "Yes," "Please," and "Thank You." These words put in that combination are magical. If you can manage to use these three words with every man you date, you will already be a step above.

Do not start the conversation. Do not keep a hold on the conversation. Some men's brains are slower to process; they have to think sometimes for a while before they can formulate words. Practice smiling and keep your lips tightly closed together. Do not take on idle chitchat such as "The potatoes are good, the steak is good, and those carrots… Mmmm…" Let him lead the conversation and listen carefully to what he is telling you; men will tell you lots about who they are on a first date. If a man tells you on a first date that he never wants to marry, you had better believe him. He might tell you down the line, after finding out that you want to marry that he would consider marriage, and he might very well be enchanted enough with you to consider it, but what he said first is probably closer to what his real thoughts and feelings are. It doesn't mean that he won't ever marry you, he might, but you will have to be more than vigilant in reeling this one in.

Be charming, appreciative, and thankful. Men are very simple in their expectations from a woman. A simple "Thank you for a most beautiful evening" will get you much farther than an exposé on your job's responsibilities and exploits.

I no longer need to do, I simply have to be. Amen.

16

Being Receptive, Appreciative, Positive and Accepting

To make the world a friendly place, one must show it a friendly face.

James Whitcomb Riley

BY BEING RECEPTIVE ON YOUR DATES, you will allow the flow of generosity from men to get to you. Too often the first word that comes out of a woman's mouth is "no." "No" is an important word to say when you need to convey that you will not go along with something that makes you feel uncomfortable. However, saying things like "I don't like camping," or "I never want to go back to Mexico," or "I don't like beach resorts" is not something that should come out of your mouth on a date.

You might not have liked the camping trip you went on fifteen years ago, or you might have had a bad experience in Mexico twelve years ago, and you might have disliked the crowded beach resort you went to last year. However, this new man might take you to the best camping trip ever with caviar and champagne, take you to Mexico where you would be pampered, wined and dined while being serenaded until the early hours of the morning, or he might even want to take you to his beach resort in Hawaii!

If asked something like, "Have you ever been camping

before?"—and only if he asks—answer something like "Yes, I have." A man might ask you, "Did you like it?" Please do not go into great details about how much you hated the trip, but say something like, "Well, it was very interesting to say the least. We arrived at the campground late during the afternoon, and they only could give us a spot on the outskirts of the campground. I wish I could try it again and have a nicer experience." Voila! You sounded grounded and open to try it again. One man you date might tell you, "I understand, I don't like camping myself, I only like to stay in five-star hotels when I travel around the world, and when in Paris and London, I stay at the apartments I own there; while in Rome, I stay at the St. Regis Grand Hotel. I am sure you would love the St. Regis, it is one of my favorites…" Or another man might say, "Great, I am glad you want to try it again, because every year I go on a two-week camping trip with a group of my friends. We all rent comfortable motor homes, and we travel through a few states we haven't seen before. It is a lot of fun and a great occasion to spend time with a dozen of my long time good friends. We travel in style; I think you would like it!" Excellent! On both dates you came out as a winner and might end up going camping with "camping guy" AND ALSO going to Rome with "five-star hotel guy!"

I promise, on my honor, to keep an open mind when I am out on a date. So help me God.

SHOWING APPRECIATION

Masculine men love to give, protect and cherish the women in their lives. They also want to be appreciated by the women in their lives. Men are very uncomplicated, and a simple "thank you" will take you a long way. Be appreciative of the things men do for you. From a simple gesture of getting you sugar from the store because he knew you ran out of it and have been too busy to get more, to him getting you that new ski mask you raved about, do not be shy voicing your appreciation to men. Men feed on appreciation, and they melt over it. You have everything to gain by letting a man know you appreciate him and what he does for you.

If you are a decent enough cook, make him some food to take home with him. Most men will be very proud to show up at work with a homemade meal his date made for him the day before. And if you did not actually make that homemade-tasting pecan pie, make sure you throw the box away before he shows up. He will love that piece of pie even better thinking you made it with him in mind. This is not cheating; this is marketing yourself well. If you knit and know that he would love a new ski hat, go ahead and make one especially just for him.

You do not need to spend a lot of money on men for them to be happy. They are much easier to please than we are. Just make sure that you show them appreciation for their actions towards you.

BEING POSITIVE

Having a positive attitude is learned and practiced. With the pressures of life, we often find ourselves too busy and frustrated as we get too many bombarding situations we need to deal with on a daily basis. Make a point to start thinking at least a positive thought every day, such as, "Today I will accept that the neighbors' kids are noisy while playing, and it is nice to see them so alive," "Today I will smile at the janitor at work and ask him how his day's going," "Thank you, God, for one more day," and so on. There are good books about positive thinking you might want to acquire and read. Norman Vincent Peale said: "Change your thoughts, and you change your world."

Being positive about your life will also help you to live in the moment. Also, when you choose positive thinking as a way of life it will become a habit, and it will have positive effects upon you and the people around you.

In the beginning, it is not easy to shed the nagging negative thoughts that ultimately bring you down. But keep in mind that for the most part, the negative thoughts and actions you entertain towards you and others were initially learned. And what was learned can be changed and adapted to the new you and your new life. You can change whatever you want, and you can achieve anything you want.

The only thing you need to do in order to change your thoughts is start replacing one negative thought for one positive thought. It might take you a few days or a few weeks. Keep working on it until you no longer are thinking that particular negative thought. Then, move onto another negative thought and replace it for a positive one. Take the necessary time for your brain to re-map itself, and you will soon realize that the more you train your brain to entertain positive thoughts versus negative ones, the easier and faster it will be for you to achieve the transition from negative to positive.

You will love the new you and others will too. Men will want to be around a beautiful, spirited woman such as you. Change yourself, and you will change the world around you. You will be happier and smile bigger, I promise you that.

Make this transformation from negative to positive thinking a conscious effort in your life every day, and you will see beautiful changes happening to you and all around you.

I promise, on my honor, to change one negative thought for a positive thought as often as I can. So help me God.

ACCEPTING WITH GRACE

Accepting is often a difficult thing for women to do these days. Women have learned to provide for themselves, and they often think that they owe a man who gives to them. You do not owe anything more than respect, kindness and appreciation to a man who does for you and gives to you. Accepting gracefully might take practice for you, which again will make multiple dating even more valuable to you. Practice makes perfect.

When a man wants to give to you, either by wanting to put new tires on your car or getting you a plane ticket to visit your sister who lives far away, instead of saying, "Oh, no, I could not accept that," just practice biting your tongue and then opening your mouth and saying, "Thank you. This is so generous of you. I appreciate it and I gladly accept. Thank you." You will see him proudly puff up because he has known how to please you. He will be happy with himself for having known how to make you happy.

Men, by nature, are very generous and giving. It is in their nature to give. You are doing men a favor by accepting their offering and letting them give to you. And your giving back to them will give them the fuel they need in order to give you even more.

Treat men lovingly and accept what they want to do for you or give to you, unless, of course, it would hurt your person or your property, in which case then just say, "Thanks, but no thanks."

*I promise, on my honor, that I will gracefully accept the
bounty men will bestow onto me. So help me God.*

• • •

Here's an example of how to stay receptive, appreciative, positive and accepting even with a man who has broken up with you and is still calling.

Dear Fléchelle,
My boyfriend and I broke up five weeks ago. He calls me daily to ask how I am and to chat. He doesn't ask me out. Today he said that one of his friends told him he saw my dating profile online, and asked me how this was going. I didn't know what to say. I babbled and it made me feel uncomfortable. How should I handle his asking me such questions? Rose

Dear Rose,
Tell him: "Oh, very well. Thank you for asking…" You answer these questions the same way you would answer his asking you "How's your mother?" Chances are he won't ask you anymore how well things are going for you! Congratulations on keeping

the line of communication open with him. The fact that he asks you these types of questions means that he still cares for you. If you like him, keep him around; who knows what's going to come out of it? Keep up the good work!

17

Respecting Men

*There is no respect for others without
humility in one's self.*

Henry Frederic Amiel

A WHILE AGO I SAW ON TELEVISION a segment about a man who met his wife through a prison's Internet dating website. These dating websites cater to men and women in prison in order to help them find a mate outside prison. I was dumbfounded. If men go to prison Internet dating service to find wives, think how much more difficult it will be for women to find husbands in general. I am serious when I say that the competition is stiff out there.

Some women with whom I shared this story told me things along the line of, "Well, there has to be something wrong with these men if they cannot find a wife in the free world," or "They probably have to do it because no women want them," or "They must be very controlling." Well, masculine men are very controlling by nature, but I was not ready to accept the idea that some men went to prison to find wives because there was something wrong with these men.

One basic thing a man needs from a woman in order to marry her is respect. A man needs to be respected. Most women think it is sex that makes a man marry a woman; think again. I know more men who are with women with whom they have no sex, than men who are with women who have no respect for them. In the long run, men are looking for admiration and appreciation much more than they are looking for sex.

So why is finding wives in a prison Internet dating service an alternative for men? In their need to be appreciated and respected, men are looking for women who need them. Some women in prison, I am sure, are very appreciative of having a man waiting for them and having a home to go to. I would think such women would be incline to be responsive and respect a man who would want to love and protect them. The guest couple that was on the television show was a loving normal-looking couple with the difference that she was not bickering at him but looked up to him with respect and appreciation. He was her hero. Get it?

Respecting and appreciating a man is so basic that it would seem simple to remedy, right? Wrong. I get phone calls from women who tell me they know men who need my help in order to be "fixed." I always smile at that one, because I know that it is often much easier to put the blame on others instead of looking at what is wrong with us. These women are surprised to hear me say that, on many occasions, I do not find that it is the men who have the problem, but in fact, that it is the women!

Women once respected their men and were proud of them. How often do you hear single women these days say that they admire a man they know in their family, at work or at their gym? How often do you see single women acting respectfully towards men? Start respecting men, and you will see them transform into real gentlemen. A man is a man until he meets a lady, then he becomes a gentleman. Ladies, please respect men. Stay ladylike so that men are motivated to act as gentlemen around you.

What if you would practice—while out with your dates— looking at them with admiration? Yes, you heard me right: admiration. You know what it looks like to give your undivided attention to the person talking with you? Just do it. When your date is talking to you, look him in his eyes and have an approving smile on your face. The smile on your face will let him know you approve of him, and he will talk to you more and more wanting to please you, which in turn will make you both happier. Think "Southern Belle!"

You will gain tremendously by giving your admiration and respect to a man. Not only will it turn him into the kind of man you say you never meet, but also it will allow you to grow respect for that man, and it will soften you in equal amount to the empowerment he will gain from you.

It might be hard at first to get to that vulnerable stage (of looking up to a man) if you are a well accomplished independent woman. Let's face it, the more accomplished we become, the harder it is not to develop into egocentric beings. Humility is a valuable attribute that is learned and practiced. Humility is a beautiful and endearing quality that is well worth acquiring. Humility allows interdependence to flourish, and interdependence is a key component in any conscious loving relationship.

You want to be with a man in a loving and caring relationship, right? So how about setting aside all your assets while on a date? How about walking into that restaurant and making it so that only you and your date are sitting at the table? No more accomplishments, no more BMW's and Rolexes. No more ex-boyfriends, ex-husbands, ex-lovers—just you and he. Give it a try. Be that twenty-something fun girl you used to be before life made you who you are today. You have nothing to lose.

The price women pay today for decades of competition with men is being single. Men do not want to be bothered with women who have nothing else to talk about other than criticizing them and telling them how bad they did this or that.

My advice to you is to respect men. If you already respect men, great; keep up the good work. If you like to bash men while out with your girlfriends, stop. It is only a bad habit that won't bring you happiness. You can discipline yourself by stopping yourself as soon as you are making a snide comment about men. You can discipline any bad habits if you want them vanished enough. Men sense women who are disrespectful, and they stay away from them. I am sure that you can find better things to do than bashing men. On the positive side, you'll start meeting great men. How bad can that be?

· · ·

18

Treating Men With Kindness ~ Breaking Up With Gentleness

*Be kind, for everyone you meet is
fighting a hard battle.*

Phito

IF, AFTER MUCH SOUL SEARCHING, YOU HAVE DECIDED that a man you have been dating is not a contender for you, and you want to break up with him, I suggest you to do it with as much gentleness as possible.

The best way to turn a man down in a humane manner is not to tell him there is something wrong with him, such as, "You're too young," "You're too old," or "You're too short..."

A better way to let go of men without damaging them and their egos is to tell them something like, "Someone from my past has come back into my life, and I want to give this relationship a chance." This won't bruise their egos, and most of them will even wish you good luck. They will probably ask you to call them if you ever become available again. When you break up with men, please *never* tell them it is because of their shortcomings. It won't serve you well, and it won't serve them well either.

If, after having seriously investigated and negotiated a future married life with a fiancé, you find that you want to break up with him and move on with your life, first thank him for all he has done for you and tell him that after having felt your feelings regarding marrying him, you have found that you do not feel right about moving onto a marriage with him. If he wants to argue with you, just tell him that your feelings are not negotiable, and that you hope he understands your feelings. Don't try to justify why you do not want to marry him; the fact that you do not want to marry him is enough of a good reason not to marry and to break up with him.

Why do I insist on letting a man down as gently and as humanely as possible? Because I love women and I want to protect them in the future with my actions of today. See, when you bruise men, you bruise their gentle souls and bruised men cannot do as well with the women they meet in the future. When you tell men you do not want to see them anymore because there is something wrong with their person, or personality trait, it hurts them, as there is nothing they can do about it, and then they carry this hurt with them into their next relationship. So, I believe it best not to hurt men in order to protect women! Ladies, please protect other women from being hurt by damaged men by minimizing the damage you do to men. Will you?

Our actions have repercussions on other people's lives, hence the importance of acting in a most conscious and gentle way. Emily Post encapsulated well the meaning of "Do good unto others" when she said, "Manners are a sensitive awareness of the feelings of others. If you have that awareness, you have good manners, no matter what fork you use."

Adopting a loving way of life will enhance all of your relationships. It will enhance your relationship with your family, friends, co-workers, and everybody else you will encounter. Try to see it this way: how would you be with people if you were only five years old, and life had not impaired you yet? You would certainly have a much more positive outlook on life than what you have now, wouldn't you say? You can keep in your heart that youthful feeling of kindness towards other people and especially towards men. You will need all the help you can get, because I know how challenging men can be. However, I promise that if you treat men with kindness and no hidden agendas, you will transform the men in your life into gentlemen—the type of men you will be proud of, instead of the kind of men you'll just want to step all over.

I want to share with you the following story because I think it demonstrates well that, in reality, many hurt feelings between men and women stem from women's misconceptions of men.

I took a psychology class in which we were given an assignment to find out about misconceptions between the sexes and the ways men and women thought of each other. It was quite an eye opener. The men and women were to do their assignments in separate rooms.

Each group was to write on a flip chart what they thought of each other. Then, on another flip chart, they were to write what they thought the other group thought of them.

I was, of course, sitting in the women's group, and one of the students was assigned to write all the words on the flip chart that were said out loud from all of the other female students. I was amazed at the words women used to describe men. They used words such as "pigs," "jerks," "stupid," and many more atrocious words I won't repeat here. I was the only one in the class brave enough to use words such as "protectors," "generous," "warm," "loving," "caring," and so on. At some point, a young lady turned towards me and said, "Wow, I would like to know where you meet such men!" I thought of that remark, and realized that it was not so much that I met different men, it was just that I acted in ways that made men want to be protective, generous, warm, loving and caring. I realized that I brought the best out of men, and it was probably the reason why I liked men so much. If I thought men were jerks and other such bad attributes, I guess I would not like them either.

When it was time to write down the attributes they thought men would say about them, the words they wrote down were not much more positive than the ones they used to describe what they thought of men.

When the assignment was completed, the men were brought back into the room along with their own flip charts. The men came in all smiling and obviously had a very good time doing their assignment.

The women first started by reading out loud the words they had written that described what they thought of men. The men soon lost their smiles, as you can just imagine.

Then it was the men's turn to read out loud what they had written about women. The men wrote much more positive words about the women. They wrote words such as "soft," "beautiful," "sexy," "nice," "smell good," along with word such as "princesses," "bitches," and "big spenders," but the majority of their thoughts regarding women were very positive and uplifting.

When it came time to share the words used to describe what they thought the other group thought of them, once again the disparity was gigantic. The men thought the women would say mostly good things about them, and the women thought the men would say mostly negative things about them. The men wrote mostly positive attributes, and the women mostly negative ones.

This experiment confirmed my finding that men love women and want to please them. If women were to think of men with a more positive attitude, men would then be able to meet the expectations the women would have about them. When a woman treats men with respect, she becomes the recipient of their generosity, their caring, and their love. When a woman treats men with contempt and disrespect, what she gets in return only mirrors the way she treats men. In a world where women are harsh with men, the men get the attitude of "It's every man for himself," and they will go first through the doorstep, won't open car doors, won't pull chairs, and certainly won't want to do anything positive and pleasing for women. Who can blame them?

To come back to the subject of breaking up, I suggest to keep dating your dates for as long as possible. Firstly, they are good practice, and secondly, who knows whom you can meet while out on a date with one of these men? I suggest that you keep dating all the men you date until they leave, so you won't have to continuously look for more dates. Moreover, it is bad enough to date people you are not much interested in without having to start anew all the time, so try to keep them as long as you can.

If they ask you to marry them, and you really are not interested, then you will need to let them know that you are not interested in them enough to marry. Please do it in a most gentle way, as you will, without any doubt, break their hearts. First, thank them for offering you marriage and tell them that you have enjoyed spending time with them, and although you think the world of them and think they are great men, you do not feel that you could grow deeper feelings than friendship feelings for them. Please, do not tell a man that the fact that he is too short makes it impossible for you to see yourself married to him. It would be mean to say such a thing and would not bring anything positive to him or you. Treat men the same way you would like for men to treat you.

Now, if a man asks you to marry him, and the reason you do not see yourself married to him is because you do not like to sleep with animals in your bed, and know that he sleeps with his two dogs and four cats, then by all mean tell him the real reason. You can tell him, "Joe, thank you so much for asking me to marry you. I love you very much and can definitely see a bright future with you, however, I know in my heart, that I could not have a life where cats and dogs would share the same bed with me and my husband. I hope you understand my feelings." Then shut up and let him think. If a man loves you enough, he will consider having his animals sleep somewhere else in order to have you as his wife. If he likes his animals more than you, than you are better off knowing it as soon as possible.

Do not tell a man the true reason of your wanting to break up with him if it is for something he cannot change, such as being bald, short, fat, skinny, with a speech impediment, and so on. If it is possible for him to change whatever bothers you, such as you do not like a beard, or do not like his house, then share your feelings with him, when the time is right, after you have asked him the permission to speak with him about your concerns.

Ladies, again, please do not forget to thank a man for all he has done for you. Do it from the bottom of your heart. Send him back into the world a better man for having known you.

19

What To Talk About On A Date ~ The First Date

*Debate is masculine, conversation
is feminine.*

Amos Bronson Alcott

KEEP THE CONVERSATION LIGHT AND BREEZY. No need to share your inner thoughts about alien visitors or world politics. Not all masculine men like to control the flow of the conversation, but most of them do. If they are not interested in what you are saying and change the subject without prior warning, do not think that they do not like you, they might just be disinterested in what you are saying at the time and think it best to just change the subject. Not all men can stomach your friend Mary's birth delivery story while eating a plate of beef bourguignon. Have you ever felt after a date that you might have talked too much? Please try to say as little as you can.

Because in the end you are the one with the power to say yes or no to men's offers, let the men interview you instead of your interviewing them. A man's job is to interview the women he goes out with because it is his responsibility to make sure that the woman will fit *his* life. He is the one who will ask you to marry him and join him to share his life and lifestyle, so let him do the interviewing on the first few dates. You will have many chances to find out about him by listening to him and by answering his questions. You will have plenty of time to ask him your pertinent questions later on. At this point, you do not need to interview him, you only need to listen to find out if he is the type of man you are looking for and if he has the type of life you would like to belong to. Of course, this applies to you even more if you want to have children, stay home to raise them yourself, and live on his income only.

When on a date with a man, let him talk and tell you what he is thinking about. Do not try to analyze everything he says. Men are much less complex than you make them to be. During your first date, if you let him lead the conversation, you will find much about him and about his likes and dislikes. That should clue you in to the type of man he is.

If you can read between the lines, a man will tell you on the first few dates most of what you will need to know in order to find out if he is someone you would want to be courted by. Although men will tell you what they think you want to hear in order to please you, most of what comes out of their mouths on the first date is the truth. So listen very carefully. The best you can do is stay quiet and listen. Staying silent will allow you to gain knowledge.

Keep in mind, though, that words mean very little, and his actions will speak louder later on, but for now, that is all you have other than, of course, the way he treats you and others and if he opens doors, pulls chairs for you, and so on. Observe and keep a detailed record of his actions and make sure to write in your notebook all the comments or actions that lifted a red flag for you. This way, if you become enchanted with him, you will have your notes to refer to before you make the decision to be in an exclusive relationship with him or not.

If you are interested in getting married and having children and are on a date with a man who tells you he doesn't want children, believe him. Any attempts at thinking that if he would just know you better and see what a wonderful wife and mother you would be are futile. Do not waste your time and his. Just be happy you listened and you are free to make a conscious decision to move on to a better match for you.

The same applies if you are interested in being married without children and you are meeting a man whose dream is a family life with a couple of kids. Even if he is perfect for you in all other aspects, trying to make him change his mind won't work.

Pay very special attention if a man has inappropriate, aggressive or violent outburst towards you or others. These behaviors rarely change. Even with continued therapy, violent behaviors tend to get worse over time. Why would you want to be in a relationship where you would be consciously, or unconsciously, walking on eggshells? If you think you deserve a healthy relationship with a healthy man, you will get a healthy man with whom to have a healthy relationship. If you settle for a damaged, unhealthy man that is what you will get: a damaged, unhealthy man with whom you will have a chaotic relationship. Marriage is a very beautiful thing, but can be a horrible experience with an abusive man.

When men ask, be very direct in answering their questions— you do not have a hidden agenda. Make the commitment to yourself that you will tell men what it is you *really* want—not what you think they want to hear or what you think they can handle; you have to tell them *exactly* what it is you want. Men cannot read your mind, much less know what it is you really want, and most often men won't know how to ask you for what you want.

In order to do that, you need to know both what you want and what you do not want. You *want* to be married, as you do *not want* to be single anymore. You *want* to be married and have children because you do *not want* to be childless anymore. Isn't marriage or a long term relationship the reason why you are dating the way you are? If you did not want to be married, or at least be in a serious monogamous relationship, you would have a male friend for Saturday nights and some traveling companionship, and you would leave it at that, right?

Of course, you have to set your boundaries on what personal

information you want to share. You do not have to share with men any information about your past relationships, or when was the last time you had sex, or about your financial assets. You can tell them you do not feel comfortable discussing these subjects with men you barely know. Do not be shy to tell them just that. At this time, questioning you on your sex life or on your finances would be totally inappropriate. It is better to let them know from the beginning that you have well-established boundaries.

To come back to the subject of answering men's questions directly, here are a few examples of what you might want to practice saying in front of a mirror to answer questions such as "What is it you are looking for?"

- I am looking to be married.

- I am looking to be married and have children.

- I am looking to be in a long-term relationship.

- I am looking to be in a monogamous relationship.

Practice any of these, or all of these (or any others of your choice) in front of a mirror as much as you can, as it will make it easier for you to say these words when the time comes for you to answer such questions. I know it is hard for many women to tell men that they ultimately want to be married and have children as they are afraid it will make them sound desperate. Men will not think that you are desperate; they will just hear what you are telling them as valuable information. Men are so much more direct and less complicated than we are. Do not think that it is better for you to tell men that you don't know what you want and are just looking to see where "things" will take you. Although you might think that it will sound friendlier to men, the fact is that marriage minded men prefer women who know what they want. If what you want is not in their agenda, they'll let you know. Better sooner than later, wouldn't you agree?

Dating all eligible men who ask you out will also make you practice being quiet and teach you how to listen. When you meet a good match, you will know usually within the first three dates. Should a man not impress you on your first date, please give him at least three dates before you decide he is not the man for you unless, of course, he does or says something that would be considered illegal, unethical or immoral.[2] Illegal means that it could put you in trouble with the law, unethical means it could damage your money and your property, and immoral could put your life or your physical, moral and emotional health at risk. For example, you might tell a man you won't see him again because you do not like the fact that he robs banks for a living, but keep your mouth shut if it is only that you do not like the ties he wears. Keep in mind that they are all only practice until one of them takes you off the market.

Again, keep your mouth shut as much as you can. You will have the chance to ask questions later. Remember that women are the gatekeepers and have the veto right to say yes or no to any offers coming their way. If you keep in your mind the reality that you are the one in the end who will choose the man you want, you will be able to stay in control of yourself while dating, which will consistently empower you and keep you on the right track.

Keep reading the list of commitments you have made for yourself; you will get what it is you want by intently focusing on it with your thoughts and your actions.

A big plus about not talking so much is that you won't be so tired after a date, and you will want to date more. There is nothing more tiring for a woman than to try to keep a man interested by babbling all night long. Let him want to keep you interested.

All you have to do is look good, smell good, smile, be receptive, and have fun. Do not forget to thank them for the food and the good time you have had with them. Men are very simple. They just want to know that you are interested and would want to see them again.

•　　•　　•

Dear Fléchelle,
I was out on a sixth date with a man and found myself annoyed again with the fact that he keeps cutting me off in the middle of my stories. He just changes the subject and starts talking about something else. I like him a lot as he is really the type of man I have been looking for, but I feel that he doesn't respect my opinions. What should I tell him so that he stops cutting me off and starts listening to me? Lucille

Dear Lucille,
How long have you been looking for a man like him—a man who is your type and whom you like? Probably a long time. I suggest you stop telling him your stories. Obviously, he is not interested in them. Dear, will you please respect him and follow his lead? Let him lead the conversation, and you will find what he likes to talk about; make weekly appointments with your girlfriends so you can tell them all the stories you want. I am sure that there are some things he likes about you since he keeps calling you and taking you out on dates. I suggest you cultivate what it is he likes in you and keep him around. Be happy to have finally been found by a man who, although he doesn't like your stories, enjoys your company. Good luck!

20

What To Wear On A Date

*A woman's clothes should be
conservatively sexy: showing enough
to arouse interest while discreet
enough to cover the essentials.*

YOU WANT TO LOOK THE BEST YOU CAN. A woman does not need
to look like a supermodel to be loved by a man. Wear clothes
that will make you look classy. If you show some legs, wear a
more conservative top. If you show some cleavage, wear a more
conservative bottom. Do not overwhelm a man on your first date
with all of your physical attributes. Keep him wondering. If
you are a very beautiful woman and know that men are usually
intimidated by your looks, then wear a nicely cut pant suit,
something simple and classy, and pretend you don't see him drool
from the corner of his mouth while on your date; he will recover.

Although we are bombarded with magazines that tell us on
a daily basis how to dress like a sex kitten for men, that has not
helped any woman get a husband. You should look nice and
sexy without looking like a working girl. Although dressing
like a Victoria Secret's model might look appealing to you, it
would send mixed signals to your dates. Dressing attractively
but modestly is your best choice while dating. Modesty means to

be reserved in matters of dressing, speaking and behaving. The way you dress is an outward sign of how you think of yourself inwardly. Pure and simple.

Men will react to your words and what you wear. If your goal is to be married, the way you dress along with your attitude and your words will say that you are serious. Your looking sexy with modesty will send the signal that although you are a sexual being, you are not into giving him a quick fix at the end of the evening. Men will know that in order to have you, they will need to go through the process of properly courting you. The serious contenders will have to go the extra mile in order to get a quality woman such as you.

Give a chance to the man sitting in front of you to look you over by looking down at your menu for a little longer than you usually would. Slowly move your eyes back to him so he has a chance to unglue his eyes from your chest before you catch his eyes. Especially if you are well endowed, men love to look at women's breasts, and the man sitting in front of you is probably no exception. So give him the chance to get it out of his system early in the date.

If a man invites you to a formal dinner or a gala, and you are unsure of the dress code, it is proper for you to ask him what is the dress code. If he doesn't know, ask him to check with the people organizing the event and let you know, as you do not want to be over or under dressed.

Beware of men who will ask you to dress sexy on a date. If a man tells you how to dress on a date (unless he is telling you that the event he is inviting you to is a black tie affair, and you may wear a gown), then there is something wrong with this man.

A client of mine was invited by a man to join him along with his mother and aunt to the opera on their first date. She gladly accepted. On the day of the date he called her, she thought, to give her the directions to the opera hall. Instead, he gave her directions to his business and asked her to meet him there at seven o'clock. She did not feel very good about meeting him at his work place, since his business was in an exclusively commercial area of town and would certainly be deserted at seven o'clock on a Friday night.

She was going to tell him that she would have felt more comfortable meeting him at the opera hall when he told her to wear something sexy with high heels. Now, why would a man want a woman to wear something sexy with high heels on their first date, albeit to the opera, where she would also meet his mother and aunt? And he wanted her to meet him in a deserted part of town?

By that time she was turned off by him, but decided to keep her engagement, and told him that she would feel more comfortable meeting him at the opera and asked him for the name of the opera hall and directions. He told her that he wanted her to meet him at his place of business as he wanted to drive together to the opera. She told him again she would feel more comfortable meeting him at the opera, and he told her that she either meet him at his place of business or he would not see her at all.

She thanked him for the invitation but decided to decline. Her instinct probably saved her life.

Again, the way you dress while out on dates is very important. Your clothes project who you are, what you want, and what you do not want. Keep it nice and simple or extravagant if you prefer, but make sure that your clothes set forth what your ultimate intentions are.

21

I Don't Feel The Chemistry

*Sexiness wears thin after a while and
beauty fades, but to be married to a
man who makes you laugh every day,
ah, now that's a real treat.*

Joanne Woodward

GOOD HUSBANDS DO NOT ALL LOOK LIKE GQ MODELS. They range
from tall and skinny, short and fat, tall and bald, short and bald,
good looking, great looking, funny looking, to strange looking.

Do you think that the beautiful, slim, tall, and elegant woman
you saw the other night felt instant chemistry for the short, bald,
average looking man who was opening the car door for her the
first time she saw him? You saw that sparkling ring and wedding
band she was wearing didn't you? Her husband was also wearing
a wedding band and seemed really proud of his beautiful wife, did
he not? Did you wonder at that moment why it was not you sitting
in that luxurious car being catered to by a man just the way this
man was treating his wife? If you felt a pang of jealousy at that
moment, you would be a normal woman in her thirties or perhaps
forties desperately looking for a husband.

Feminine women do not feel instant chemistry for men.
Women in touch with their femininity do not develop chemistry
with a man because of the way he looks; they develop chemistry

151

for a man because of what he does for them. Your body might love a man's body, but instant chemistry has been known to create little more than havoc in many women's lives.

Men grow on us. Again, we feel love towards men because they do things for us, not because they look good. It is an advantage for a woman not to be too attracted to a man at the onset. It helps men fall in love with you if you are not too physically attracted to them because they have to work harder to get you. They have to chase harder, and they have to do more for you. Men love to do for women and appreciate women who will let them do for them.

Think back to all the men you were very attracted to when you first met them. Have any of them turned out to be good men who cared for you and cherished your feelings? Or were they not, in fact, men you had to continuously chase in order to get their attention?

I know women who are married to wonderful men with whom they had no or very little chemistry in the beginning of their courtship. So be careful about not seeing a man because he doesn't knock your socks off. It is much better to be with a man who doesn't drive your hormones too wild too fast. Believe me, it will keep you virtuous longer, therefore giving him the chance to truly fall in love with you.

Go out with a man at least three times. Of course, if he is rude, belligerent, or a bully, then you do not need to see a man any longer after the initial date. The same goes if he has smoked marijuana in his car on the way to pick you up, and you have decided not to date anyone who consumes drugs. *Capish?* However, if a man is a gentleman with you, treats you well, respect you, and cares for you, then see him at least, at a very minimum, three times. And if you have nothing better to do, I would suggest you keep on dating him for as long as he wants to date you. You never know, maybe months later, if you haven't found anyone better than he, he may be the best man for you after all. And again, as you already know, you never know whom you can meet while out on a date!

There are many types of chemistry: physical, emotional, spiritual, intuitional, and more. While having physical chemistry is an important component to any good relationship, a relationship will not endure if the other components needed for a good relationship are non-existent. Primarily, I believe that it is more important to feel loved, cherished, and safe in a relationship with a man. The sparks will come when you are with a man who will tell you and prove to you by his commitments towards you that he wants to take care of you, cherish you and protect you. The sparks will grow when he proves to you that he will handle things so that you do not have to worry, and you can stay home, flourish, and have a family.

I would not worry too much about going out with a man you do not feel chemistry with. However, if after three dates, you still would not be able to see yourself *ever* kissing him—even after he has flown you in his private jet to take you out to dinner in San Francisco, followed by a night at the opera, has given you diamonds on your second date and written poems with your name all over them, and thinks that you are the most beautiful creature he has ever seen—well, if you absolutely must, then just tell him that, unfortunately, you simply do not feel chemistry for him. And do not worry about him, he'll find someone who will appreciate a man like him really soon!

If you are not attracted to a man and have no chemistry for him, look at your plate a lot, and say, "Uh, huh! Uh, huh!" It will keep you from talking too much and will help you to practice your dating skills and learn more about men. Dating multiple men, even the ones you are not attracted to, will keep you busy and will keep you from thinking too much about the ones you like. Diversity is a good thing when you are looking for a husband.

Real chemistry for me is something you have with a man with whom you can be yourself. A man you can talk to, a man with whom you do not feel that you have to walk on eggshells. Real chemistry is being with a man who makes you feel good about yourself.

A woman can have an excellent sexual relationship with a man she felt no attraction towards in the beginning of their courtship. Being attracted to a man does not assure you a great relationship;

however, going out with men whom you are not initially attracted to might get you an excellent husband in the end. How will you know if a man would be a good husband unless you give him the chance to prove himself to you?

Because most women think that they need to be initially attracted to a man in order to accept a date, many women pass on the chance to find a good husband solely based on the man's looks. Now that you have read this, I am sure that you realize that it is rather shallow to deprive a man the opportunity to date you because he doesn't fit your physical standard, right? And what would happen if you would marry your perfect physical standard man and later on, he was in a car accident and became dismembered or disfigured? Would you leave him for not fitting the idea of what you find acceptable for a man to look like?

There is a reason why our mothers, grandmothers and mothers before them say that it is better to be with a man who loves us more than we love him. Being wanted feels much better than wanting.

If women would stop idealizing "instant chemistry," they would be much better off emotionally. Most women want chemistry because they are used to the rush they get when they are with a man who is with them for their sex and physical body. The other side of the coin is that this is a man she is always afraid to lose. He is with her for her sex, not herself. And sex is everywhere.

A marriage minded man is looking for more than a lover when looking for a wife, so his approach might be slower than what you are used to. However, when a woman is with a man who is with her for herself, she is not worried about losing him. She knows she is unique to him, and can feel relaxed in her relationship with that man.

The happiest women are married to men who love them for who they are as women, not because they provide a constant sexual flow. These happy women might not have felt chemistry for their husbands until much later in their relationships.

Women who choose sex as their primary criteria to select a mate often get just that: sex. But in the long run, a woman is much happier when choosing a man because he loves and cherishes her, instead of choosing a man because she is attracted to him. And the chemistry will kick in once you have sex with the right man for you anyway. Haven't you ever started feeling chemistry for a man you did not care much about until after you had sex with him? The oxytocin bonding will work its wonders when you are with a good man as well as it did in the past with bad ones. Besides, if you have never tried to wait in order to have sex with a man before he first fell in love with you and committed himself to you and to your happiness, you will be surprised at how wonderful and safe you will feel. And this can be a possibility for you if you are not too attracted. Long ago, mothers would tell their daughters to wait before having sex, because sex was better after (marriage) than before. What they meant was not that the sexual connection would be better, but that the chemistry is better balanced when all the elements of love, affection, and commitments from both partners are in place.

When I hear women say: "I like him, he is such a nice man, but he is not a good kisser," I always ask them the same thing: "Do you want to be with a man who will make you feel good in bed, or do you want to be with a man who will be a good provider for you and your future children?" You cannot have it all. Good providing men are often too tired to perform. They most certainly won't perform as well as the surfer dude you used to go out with. Besides, the surfer dude had you pay for half the meal ticket, if you were not actually paying for both of you, right? You have to ask yourself, "Do you want great sex or a good husband for yourself and a great father for your children?"

Anyway, if what you really want is a husband in order to build a life and have children with, whom you intend to raise yourself instead of having day care do it for you, I don't see why you would want to be all hot and bothered with a man until he has proposed to you, has informed you of his intentions towards you, and has financially secured a future for you and the children you'll stay home to raise. Does this make sense to you?

Of course, to get the type of relationship you want, then you will need to use common sense and judge for yourself what it is you need from a man. Just make sure that you get what you want and choose wisely if you intend to bring children into this world. A little planning might make the difference between children being raised with or without their dad.

And again, if all you want is great sex, then his willingness to have sex with you is all you'll need. But before you let go of a man because you do not feel chemistry with him, visualize this next scenario:

Just imagine that it is five years later, and you are still single and dating. You have had high hopes and low despairs quite a few times in the last five years. One of your dates has invited you to a barbecue at his friend's house. It is Sunday afternoon, and your date picks you up and drives you to his friend's house. You go through a pretty neighborhood with well-manicured lawns.

Your date parks the car in front of a lovely house, and you wonder what his friend does for a living. You both walk along a rose-lined path to the front door. A beautiful and gracious woman opens the door and warmly greets you both. You walk inside this very beautiful house and are smiled at by two of the cutest, happiest looking children.

Your date takes you by the arm and walks you to the backyard to meet his friend who's roasting chickens and beef briskets on an open fire pit. Everything you see around you is exactly what you want for yourself. Your date's friend turns around, and you recognize him: he is a man whom you told you did not feel chemistry with after just a few dates. He greets you with warmth and welcomes you into his home.

Along with feeling grateful that he did not recognize you, you are feeling more alone and lonely than before. It could have been you, but no. You are a thirty-something-year-old woman who is still single, looking for a husband in order to build a family.

22

Sharing Your Love With A Man

You give but little when you give of your possessions. It is when you give of yourself that you truly give.

Kahlil Gibran

AN ANCHORED FEMININE WOMAN LOVES HERSELF FIRST and then shares that love with a man worthy of her love.

An anchored feminine woman does not fall in love with a man. As the word correctly describe it, "falling" in love does not foretell much uplifting coming out of such an action. An anchored feminine woman elevates people around her with the love and the respect she harbors inside herself. She can achieve that by leading her life in a way that honors herself and allows love and respect to grow inside her and then by sharing this immense love with the people around her, including her husband, her children, her family, and those dear to her. An anchored feminine woman always puts herself first.

Most women "fall" in love with men in a way that can be better described as falling into addiction. Oxytocin is most often what makes these women think they are "in love" rather than have "love" for a man. Women often are with men they know they should not be with and say that they cannot leave them because they are already "in love."

Understanding the concept of sharing love as opposed to falling in love makes it easier not to fall into addiction.

When does a woman share the love she has for herself with a man? When he has proven to her the level of his dedication towards her and their relationship by giving her what she needs and wants.

Do men deserve to receive love from a woman if they don't call when they said they would or if they don't keep the commitments they made to her? Do men deserve being the recipient of a woman's love when she catches him lying, cheating, drinking, and drugging? Should a woman give her love to a man who disrespects her and has no regard for her? No. A woman will share the love she has for herself with a man who has proven himself worthy to receive such a gift.

Good men tell me all the time they think that women do not like good men, that in fact they really think they prefer the "bad boys." They do not understand why women give them the cold shoulder and are with men who disrespect them, cheat on them, lie to them, and steal from them.

I explain to these good men that women get bonded to these bad men through the bonding effect that is created when oxytocin is released during sexual intimacy they have with these men. I tell them that these women have not been vigilant enough to keep the gate closed to men until such time as these men have proven themselves worthy of their time, love, affection, and energy. These women incur great risks to find themselves in painful long-term relationships with these bad men. Bad men know how to keep their women bonded by keeping them on a high level of oxytocin by having sexual encounters on a regular basis. Bad men will give their women the fix (sex) they need at least once a week. Bad men know that when women decide to stop having sex with them that they are in trouble as she is escaping their spell. Smart and informed women will make sure that they do not fall prey to men who want nothing more from them than having sex without having to commit or do anything for them.

A feminine woman has everything to gain in protecting her oxytocin-susceptible self from men who haven't first given her the commitment she needs.

When do we share the love we have within ourselves with a man? When he has informed us by his actions of his intentions to be there for us, love us, cherish us, and protect us. Then, there is nothing more wonderful than to share with them what God has given us in abundance.

Men are as good as women require them to be. Take care of yourself, and love yourself first. When they have shown you through their commitment that they are worthy of receiving the kind of love you have for yourself, then you can share your love in ways which you are comfortable with.

Would you please consider not loving a man until he is in love with you? It takes men much longer to fall in love. Then why not let the man fall in love with you and pursue you as if you were the last woman on earth for him? Then you insure yourself to be with a man who really wants you, versus being with a man you really want and will have to chase forever. Real men are attracted to women who are centered and love themselves first.

Women do not fall in love. Women share the love they have for themselves with the men of their lives, their families and their friends.

I promise, on my honor, that I will not love a man better than I love myself. So help me God.

. . .

Part Four

Getting The Task Underway

. . .

23

How To Get Dates

*Everything you want is out there
waiting for you to ask. Everything you
want also wants you. But you have to
take action to get it.*

Jules Renard

NOW THAT YOU ARE LOOKING THE PART and have an idea of what you want, let's look at your options regarding where to go and what to do in order to be in the proximity of the coveted prize, your future husband.

Along with the conventional ways of meeting people such as at bars, restaurants, grocery stores, bookstores, and so on, there are also a wide variety of dating agencies. I listed a few different types of services you might want to inquire about. Before you sign up with any of these agencies, make sure that you have interviewed them and found that the quality of people they work with is equal to what you are looking for. There are some classy agencies out there, and there are some not too classy. If you decide to go that route, choose wisely.

DATING AGENCIES

Dating agencies specialize in finding the best possible match for you. Most will have you meet with a staff member and will ask you to give them an interview to tell them about yourself and find out what type of relationship you are looking for. It is worth the time spent as it will enhance your chance to meet the best possible match for you. Some offer the services of professional photographers that will help you look your best. Professional pictures are a big plus as men like to meet attractive women, and a professional photographer will be an important ally for you in this process. You only have one chance to make a good first impression.

Choose a dating service that can provide you with profiles and pictures. The dating service will contact you upon finding a match for you. It might be by telephone, email or fax. When you receive the profile and picture of a potential date, take the time to read it and make sure that this person is indeed a match for you. You might have told them you do not want to date men with young children, but they might have forgotten about it. So carefully study the profiles. The agency might provide you with a phone number or ask you if they can provide your telephone number to your potential date. I suggest you ask the agency to give men your telephone number and let them contact and pursue you.

Before you sign up with any of these agencies, read the small print. Some of them will offer you a certain amount of introductions for a set price with an additional charge for more introductions. Others will offer you unlimited introductions for the duration of your contract. If they give you the service you expect, they are worth the high cost they usually charge, but be aware of what will be expected from you financially before you sign the dotted line. It is also a good idea to ask for referrals. Ask them if you can speak with some of their active clients. Even if they are putting you in touch with their happiest customers, you should have a better feel for how they operate. You might also check with the Better Business Bureau to make sure that they have a clean report and are ethical in their business dealings.

PERSONAL MATCHMAKER

In general, these are the most costly of all dating services.

With a price tag up to thousands of dollars to sign up with your personal *yenta*, you definitely have to feel a *connection* with this person. If you can afford it, make sure this matchmaker will be there with you during all steps of your dating journey. From suggesting a hairstylist to the best seamstress in town, have him or her review your whole lifestyle. Make the best out of employing these professionals. As with the dating agencies, ask to speak with a few of their customers and check with the Better Business Bureau.

INTERNET DATING SERVICES

There is a large selection of Internet based dating services. Unlike the dating agencies, you make the match yourself. Most of these services will ask you to answer a selection of simple questions, which will be the basis of your profile. Your profile should describe you as accurately as possible. Questions on your height, weight, color of eyes and hair, work you do, money you make, favorite color, movies you like, and so on. After you answer the questionnaire, then you are given the chance to write something personal about yourself and about the person you are looking for. This is where you will write what it is you are looking for in a man.

The questionnaire might ask you to answer questions such as, "Please describe what you find attractive in a man and what traits are you looking for?" You could write something like "I am looking for a man who is happy, someone who loves life, appreciates the ups and is wiser for the downs, and most importantly, is not jaded by it all. I want to find a man who wants to live forever because that's exactly how long it will take to do all the things he loves and wants to do. He will be generous, kind, loving, smart, and witty. And most of all, he loves children and wants a family... Where are you?"

Or you may write something like, "I would love to meet a man who is intelligent, respectful of himself and others, and who is kind and cherishing, a man who is happy when he gets up in the morning and is thankful for another day. A man who understands and appreciates the magic of chemistry and is ready at this point in his life to commit himself to a married relationship. I am looking for the father of my future children. If you are serious about being with a woman who is committed to making a relationship work, and you want children, please write to me. I am looking forward to meeting with you."

Or something like, "I am looking for a masculine, leader type gentleman. A man who knows what he wants and is not afraid to ask for it. A man who believes that taking care of a woman's well being is not something from the past, and opening doors and pulling chairs are ways for him to express his love for the woman of his life. If you like your mother and sisters and enjoy seeing them happy, then I would love to meet you. Must be honest, open, drug free, a non-smoker, and love gourmet food and great wines."

Anything that reflects your wants and what you are looking for is acceptable here. Don't be shy, and ask for what you want. Be as realistic, frank and honest as possible about your goal. If your goal is to be married and have children, state it in your profile. This is not the time to be bashful or evasive about sharing your objectives. If you don't write precisely what it is you want, you will receive tons of letters from men who might want to be married, but do not want children, or do not want to be married, and so on. This way, you will eliminate a lot of men who would not be right for you in the first place. You won't waste your time or theirs.

I know that most of you will have qualms about directly saying that you want to be married for fear of scaring men away. The only men who will be scared away by your honesty and directness are men who are not interested in the same goals that you are, so have no fear of losing good men over this. The right men for you will be delighted by your openness and your convictions.

Now, you will also have the chance to talk about yourself. In most Internet dating services, they will ask you to describe yourself. This is where you describe the way you see yourself, and talk about your physical body and your personality. Write what it is that you like about yourself, and what makes you the confident woman you are. Something like: "I love people and parties; I love dinner parties best of all, talking late into the night, mental connections, intimacy, and spirited interplay with other human beings. I also need down time, the solitude of the Sierras, shooting wildlife photos, watching falcons fly, and long walks on the beach on a warm winter day. I can be alone but prefer to be involved in a relationship. I have loved, and I have lost and am better for all of it. I have many friends, most whom I have known for a long time, and they are men and women. I am a grown woman, but I treasure the little girl in me who never fails to be amazed at the world around her. I love children, as they are for me the source of the greatest joy in this world. I have many interests and can envision things to do for two lifetimes. I will live a long time; I can't explain why I know, but I just do. I am spiritual, yet not religious. I believe, like you, that we are all connected in a way that we may not exactly understand, but we certainly can feel. I mostly see the good in people as I care not to focus on the bad, but when it confronts me, I do not hesitate to act upon it. I am an excellent companion and like to be with a man I can respect and look up to."

Or something like: "I am 5'6", and I weigh 140 pounds; I have short brown hair and a trim body. I like to exercise and participate in many sports activities. I canoe, water-ski, snow-ski, swim, play volleyball, roller blade, mountain bike, hike, walk and dance. I like to be active mostly in the outdoors. I belong to a gym, but visit it strictly for cardio-vascular activities and weight lifting about two or three times a week. I enjoy going out for fine dining, and I also like to eat at home. I am a fairly good cook. I enjoy having friends over and sharing stories and laughter over dinner. I also love gardening; I have both a vegetable garden and a flower garden. I enjoy reading the Sunday paper sitting on the sofa while enjoying a hot coffee and cinnamon rolls."

Be open and as straightforward as possible in describing yourself.

Some Internet dating services will also give you the chance to express how you feel about other people's behavior or what you dislike about others. Be careful here, because if you write that "you find men who chew gum annoying," just keep in mind that perhaps the perfect man for you might chew gum, and coming from him, it might not be as bad as you think it might be. You would not want to alienate him just because he thinks you would not want to have anything to do with him. If you must state a dislike, be really sure that it is something you could not, for any reason or for anybody, compromise on. Something like: "I don't like people who floss at the dinner table," would definitely mean you would not be with someone who flosses at the dinner table for any reason whatsoever. "He may look like Brad Pitt, have Bill Gates' money and the intelligence of Einstein, but I will not be seen with such a man!" Get the idea? Be accepting of others. If they do something you could not live with, you'll know soon enough.

If you are separated and your divorce is pending, write in your profile that you are divorced. Men search by criteria such as single, divorced, and never married. Men, rightly so, think of a "separated" woman as a "still married" woman and think that she might be still living with her husband. After they have contacted you by phone and have voiced an interest in meeting you, then you can tell them that you wrote divorced in your profile in order to be more approachable, but that your divorce will be final on such and such a date. Keeping such information for yourself until men have had the chance to speak with you will work in your favor. As a rule, good men do not want to play around with another man's property, hence why they are reluctant to meet "separated" women. Therefore, if a man tells you that he is not interested in you until you are officially divorced, please thank him for his honesty, and tell him that he is welcome to call you back after you are legally divorced.

Keep any negative details of your life out of your profile, and do not disclose facts that would be better received from you on a face-to-face basis.

Many of the questions might not seem relevant to you, however, keep in mind that some of these sites have been developed to be a most effective tool in order for you to meet your future mate. Use these features. It will help men with similar interests find you.

I suggest that you simply put your profile on a few Internet dating sites, and let the men write to you. I find it works better when men are the pursuers. You can send them a note just to drop your "internet" hanky, but I find that the chances to successfully meet masculine men this way are very slim. Remember, masculine men like to chase, and as much as you might think that we live in a liberated world where men and women are equals, when it comes to courting, masculine men are very traditional, and it doesn't rub them the right way when women pursue them. Again, men do not like to have their energy penetrated; they want to be the ones doing the penetrating.

If you absolutely must look at men's profiles and are attracted to some of these men and would like to let them know you exist, send them a "wink" or the equivalent of an "I am interested in you," and leave it at that. If the man is interested, he will let you know. If you do not hear from him, do not pursue him. If for any reason, he does not want to go out with you, you should respect that. Consider it being the best outcome for you. There will be plenty of men interested in knowing you. Again, my suggestion is to not look at men's profiles. You might want to look at men's profiles in general, just to see what's out there, but I would let men find you instead. When you let a man know that you are interested, then half of his work is done and half the fun of chasing is gone with it. He knows he already has you, so where is the fun in winning you over?

Masculine men choose their mates with their eyes, so make sure that you post appealing pictures of yourself. Three pictures should be enough. If they want to see more of you they can contact you and arrange to meet you. Post pictures that represent you the way you look now. You can easily find companies on the Internet that for a fixed price will photograph you and provide you with digital photos for you to put into your Internet dating services profile.

Do not post pictures of you twenty pounds lighter or twenty years younger. You want to show pictures of yourself for who you are today, because this is what men will see when they finally meet you. Do not think that you are charming enough and that men will be happy to be with you even if you are a bit heavier than you led them to believe. A man's decision to write to a woman is very influenced by the way she looks in her pictures. So have recent pictures taken of you in situations that best represent you. If you are into horseback riding, post a picture of you in full gear. If your style is Gothic and you like night clubbing, then show a picture of you dressed up for a night out. Any style you are is just fine; simply make sure that you represent yourself well. Nobody likes to be misled.

Regarding your financial status, I suggest you keep it very vague, especially if you have money. There are a lot of con artists on the Internet looking especially for women with money. I suggest you hide your assets as much as possible. If you do not have any money, then don't be shy about saying so when men ask you. Masculine, provider type men won't be dissuaded by that at all.

How to respond to men who contact you through Internet dating services:

Many Internet dating services offer safe and anonymous electronic mail systems that make it easy for you to respond anonymously to men who have contacted you.

In your response letter, mention something you liked about his profile. If you read that he likes river rafting and you find this fascinating, mention it. Personalize all your letters. Please do not send pre-made form letters. Be yourself in a creative way while staying on the conservative side. You might think that something you want to write to a man about his picture sounds funny, but will sound more like an insult to him. A simple "Thank you for writing to me. I enjoyed reading your profile and would like to know more about you. Please let me know how you want for us to proceed. Looking forward to hearing from you. Carole."

Or in response to "Superman's" inquiry (his handle is Superman), you could write something like, "Dear Superman: I just finished reading your letter and your profile, and from what I read, I feel you would be someone I would like to know. I understand that you like sailing, and I do too. I am forty-one years old and you are forty-four—I like to date someone my own age who knows what a vinyl album is! ☺ (Use of signs, like a smiling face, is always welcome here.) I like poetry and so do you. I am definitely interesting in knowing more about you. You are welcome to call me at 123-456-7890. Have a most beautiful day. Susan."

Your objective is to get men on the phone with you. If men want to keep typing away as a form of communication with you, please refer to the chapter "Phone Dates, Coffee Dates, Email dates, and Hang Out Dates" in order to learn why it is not a good idea to date by email and how to respond to men in order to get them off the computer and on the phone with you so they can schedule a date with you. Use the Internet dating services as a tool to meet men, not to date men.

Do respond to men who haven't posted their pictures in their profiles. There are a lot of gorgeous single men who have no pictures posted on their profiles and married men who have theirs posted. Not wanting to date a man because you haven't seen what he looks like is just an excuse not to get dressed up and go out on dates. You are not going to have sex with them until you are engaged, so what do you care? Again, you might be waiting for your date while quietly sipping a glass of wine when the man of your life walks into that very restaurant where you have accepted to meet a five-foot-three-inch-tall, bald man!

Also, I suggest you accept dates from separated men if it is not too much of a stretch for you. Again, you are not going to have sex with a man until engaged, right? You can have plenty of dates with men who are only separated to keep your practice skills up and, of course, to have the chance to be out there and be seen!

As you know, I suggest women date "anything" that has a

heartbeat. You are not going to marry him that night, just date him. Who knows whom you will meet while waiting for your date that's late. You won't meet anybody sitting at home eating an entire cheesecake and bags of Fritos.

I know that there are weirdos everywhere, but I have had many profiles posted on the Internet, and I can say that not even one percent of the ones who contacted me were weirdos. If such men contact you, delete their emails without responding to them. Be gentle and receptive to men. Most of them have been emasculated by women and simply do not know how to properly court a woman. Be your beautiful feminine self and let them be men. You will be very surprised at what will happen when you stop trying to control everything and just sit back and enjoy receiving all that men will generously grace you with.

DATES BY THE MINUTE

These are pre-arranged dating parties where there are an equal number of men and women who pay an entrance fee in order to have the chance to sit with each and every one of the opposite sex present at the party.

You will usually be given the chance to sit down for five to ten minutes with every man present at the gathering and will have the chance to ask and answer questions.

Most women think that this is the best time to ask questions and try to know the most about the man sitting in front of them. This is the wrong approach. First of all, you want to draw the man's attention towards you. If you talk, chances are he will hear something like, "Blah, blah, blah. Blah blah, blah blah…" Then his eight minutes will be over, and he will want to move to the next woman as quickly as possible in order to recover from you.

The right thing to do is to sit silently and smile at the gentleman who sits in front of you. If it takes him a minute or two to get over your mysterious aura and gather the strength to get a word out of his mouth, who cares, there are six more minutes to go. Stay silent. There is no need for you to fill the gaps. Your job is to attract, not attack. I know it will be hard for you to just sit there silently and smile for a couple of hours, but keep in mind that the prize might be the husband you have been looking for. I am sure that thinking of it this way will make it an easier task for you.

Answer the questions asked with as much integrity as possible. Again, I know it might be hard for you to say that you are looking for a husband in order to get married and create a family, but the more you practice, the easier it will be for you to get it out of your mouth. Hence why I suggest you practice as often as you can.

So before you go to these gatherings, picture yourself sitting, smiling, and keeping an approachable and interested demeanor. Visualize the ease you will feel not to have to do anything but be receptive. Being receptive is key here. Men always have the big word "rejection" hanging over their heads. They constantly ask themselves, "Will she like me?" or "I have to be better than any other guy in here!" So be receptive and warm and don't bombard him with questions or push on him how great you are. As a feminine woman, you do not have to sell yourself; you only have to feel your feelings. You need to find out if any of the men courting you would be satisfying enough for you to give up your single status and give him the best of you for the rest of your life. Dale Carnegie said, "You can make more friends in two months by becoming interested in other people than you can in two years by trying to get other people interested in you." This is a priceless quote and a first-class way of life to adopt.

You will be given a list containing the men's names or their assigned numbers and will be given the chance to write if you want to meet with them or not. Then, later on, they will take your list and match it with the men you said you would be interested in. If these men have also written you down as a "yes" on their list, then it is a match, and you will be contacted with their email addresses or phone numbers.

Now, what will happen if you select only a few men and none of the men you selected as desirable dates have chosen you? You will have spent a whole evening smiling, spending good money to get in, ending up with no date. That is what can happen. The only remedy to that unfortunate outcome is to follow my next advice: write a "yes" beside each and every name or number of the men who sat in front of you. Even the ones you might not have had the chance to meet, at least you know that they are interested in dating. What have you got to lose? Unless the man told you that his favorite pastime is to abuse women, why would you not go out with him? In writing "yes" to all the men, you are bound to find one or two who will be interested in you and have written "yes" beside your name; therefore you haven't wasted your time and money. Do you get that system? It is a numbers game out there; make it work for you.

Again, just keep it light and fun. You'll have enough time to show the serious side of yourself in the future. You are investing in your future and are doing something that should be fun for you. Being chased can be quite addictive, you know. So, go ahead and make the best of what you are working with. A positive attitude will win you anything you want.

MEETING MEN IN PUBLIC PLACES

Going out to meet men in public places is one of my favorite ways to meet people. The places to go are countless, and you can make each and every one of your outings an opportunity to meet a potential mate.

You can go browsing in your local bookstores or in the ones in the next city. There are always a ton of men walking up and down the aisles, and they don't all look to me as if they are there shopping for books. Make yourself available with lots of eye contact. Looking at a man with an inviting smile will get you into a conversation faster than you can ever imagine. Men are looking for a sign from you saying that it is okay for them to approach you. Your smile and sparkling eyes will do it for you.

Dr. Allen says that in order to "magnetize" men to you, you look them in their eyes for a full five seconds while smiling. She says that men will trip over themselves for the chance to talk to you. She says that it can be very unnerving to keep eye contact for that long (can you imagine five full seconds!), and that you will start sweating and your upper lip might become dry and stick to your teeth, but her technique is the best I have ever tried. It worked every single time I did it. You'll feel a little naughty, but you'll get over it.

Go to any place you would feel comfortable going by yourself. Leave your girlfriends behind at least once a week to go practice your irresistible smile on men. You can practice at the gas station, especially if you fumble your way around putting gas in your car. Men will be just so happy to oblige. You can practice at the supermarket, the bowling alley, at church, and at the bank: anywhere there are male human beings around. Go for it!

Go to the dreaded singles' parties. I know how hard it is at first go to these events. You'll probably feel like a loser the first time you go, but you can make them really fun. Armed with your killer smile, your approachable and interested attitude, and your sexy walk, you will enjoy these singles' events. If you go with girlfriends, make sure that you walk around the room by yourself at least every thirty minutes. It will make you more available to the men than if they have to fend off the "pack" in order to get to you.

Just be light and have fun. Remember, men like happy women. Have fun with this.

In conclusion, you have found a great dating agency, or the most unbelievable personal *yenta*, or you've signed up onto the best computer dating service available, and you are out there flirting. Now what? The interaction begins.

. . .

24

Phone Dates, Coffee Dates, Email Dates & Hang Out Dates

Nothing builds self-esteem and self-confidence like accomplishment.

Thomas Carlyle

WOMEN TELL ME ALL THE TIME THEY DO NOT LIKE TO DATE. If they could just be introduced to the perfect man and never have to go through the ordeal of dating, they would be very happy.

Well perhaps if you knew how to date, you would like dating a little more. What do you think? What's in dating that is not to like? You go out to have dinner in fabulous restaurants, are entertained at the best shows in town, travel, and experience new things. All this while having an enthusiastic gentleman who wants to make you feel good and takes care of you! This is what "real" dating is all about.

If you want to love dating, just stay away from what makes dating seem like an ordeal to you. Following are a few pitfalls to avoid.

PHONE DATES

Many men like phone dates. Their dating method for finding

the right woman is to be vigilant and eliminate the wrong ones as soon as possible. Phone dates will eliminate you faster than you can say "Hello." Men eliminate women for a multitude of reasons as simple as the way you said something, which is exactly the way Anna, his ex, used to say it. He immediately thinks, "Oh my God! I cannot go out with this woman; she is just like Anna!" Why risk that?

Cheap men like phone dates too. What a great way to be entertained by you at the cheapest price possible.

How can you be mysterious on a phone date? How can you enchant him with your alluring smile and capture his thoughts with your heavenly body (you don't actually need to have one; men will see it this way if you think of it this way) if you are on the phone? There are no incentives for a woman to invest time in a phone date. The only thing one can do on the phone is talk, and the last thing you want to do on a date is talk. Get it? The more you talk, the faster you will be eliminated. Again, do not believe everything you are reading in magazines and see on television when they tell you that the quiet and alluring woman always loses the guys. The only guys they lose are the girly-men who need to be chased. Who needs them? You certainly don't. Chasing these men will make you hate dating. Beware of the girly-men; there are plenty of them out there, and they like to prey on women like you who are open to doing a lot when it comes to finding a husband. Do not be so desperate and think it is better to have a phone date than no date at all. Do not waste your time; a phone date is not getting you any closer to finding your husband than having no date at all.

HOW DO I SAY NO TO PHONE DATES?

It is as easy as saying "No." When your date calls you for the first time, he has prepared himself to have enough time to have a phone chat. Talk with him for five minutes, no more, and after the five minutes are over, thank him for his call and tell him you have to go. Say something like this:

You: "Well, thank you so much for calling. It was nice to hear from you. You seem like such a nice gentleman, I enjoyed our conversation. I wish you a great evening."

He: "Huh, you've got to go?"

You: "Yes, I was rushing out when you called (my dinner is ready, I have a nail appointment…)

He: "Well, can I call you again?"

You: "Sure."

He: "When?"

You: "Anytime you want. Thank you again for calling."

Say goodbye, and hang up the phone. He might book a date with you right away, or not. If not, when he calls again, keep the conversation at no more than five minutes. He will get the idea that if he wants to know you, he will need to do it face to face.

You do not want any more phone dates where you hang up the phone feeling like you've just wasted your time. Your time is precious, and your words won't serve you well unless, of course, you are looking for a girly-man, which I don't think is what you want.

During those five minutes you will talk, act interested and available. When on the first phone conversation with a man, be open, receptive, and happy. You know how to do it. You put a smile on your face before you pick up the phone and say: "Hellooooo…" through those smiling lips of yours; men pick up on these subtleties. Converse for five minutes, and then say the usual or something like this: "Thank you so much for calling; you sound like such a nice man. I was getting ready to leave when you called, but I am so happy to have had the chance to connect with you." Bang. The only things he hears are the words "nice man" and "happy." Ninety-five percent of the men will ask you to meet with them, to which you will answer: "Yes, of course, I would love to meet you." Bang. The only thing he hears is the word "love." He may ask, "What about coffee?" Just answer something like, "Thank you for inviting me for coffee; I very much appreciate it, however, I prefer to have quality time with a gentleman and like to commit to a longer date time." He might say, "Well I understand, but I don't feel good about committing myself for a full dinner," to which you answer, "Thanks, but I don't meet men for coffee dates," or he'll say "Well, what about dinner then?" Your answer to that is "Dinner sounds great. Thank you." Then you both discuss when, where, etc.

Who cares if the man sounds like a bore? You do this for practice in order to be ready so that when your man will *finally* find you, you won't fend him off with rusty dating habits. Look at your plate, and see all that beautiful food in front of you: the food you are having for dinner and for lunch the day after. As you know, always bring leftovers home with you for your lunch the day after, since you will only eat half of your meal. With all that great food out there, this is how you will keep your weight down. You cannot eat in restaurants all the time and stay slim unless you limit your food intake. Also, by eating just half of your meal, it will afford you the luxury of having dessert. If you know you won't eat the food the day after, put it in the freezer to eat at a later time.

Look at it this way: because of all the practice you will get while multiple dating, your man will find in you a refined, receptive, and appreciative woman, and, of course, he will fall in love with you, as you will truly be one of a kind, and he will want to make you his.

COFFEE DATES

I already have talked about coffee dates. Some men simply love coffee dates. These are men who want to eliminate women as fast as possible so they can move on to the next one. They are in the over-drive mode of finding the "perfect" woman, so you can just imagine how fast they'll want to go through you. Not that you are not perfect enough, just there will never be a woman perfect enough for this type of man. Coffee dates make me think that a man just wants to see the size of a woman's derrière before he invests in a meal. If the derrière does not suit him, to the next derrière he goes. You get my point?

And if you are a woman who does not want to give enough time to a man to sit through a full meal and you insist on a coffee date, please change your attitude. Do you really want to spend two hours getting ready for a thirty-minute date? Plus, by following these recommendations, you will relax enough to learn how to enjoy the company of a man for what is it: spending a fun time with someone who is planning and managing the entertainment for you. I can think of worse things that can happen during a woman's day. Wouldn't you agree?

You need to learn to respectfully reject coffee dates. If you don't reject them, you will become resentful about giving your precious time to men who are not serious enough to honor you with a decent date. Many women hate dating because they haven't learned how to say "No" to what does not feel comfortable to them.

When men offer to meet for coffee or drink dates, respectfully tell them that it is more convenient for you to meet during meal time and that you like to spend quality time with someone for at least a couple of hours over lunch or dinner. If they say no, they only meet women for coffee or drink dates, then thank them for the offer and tell them that you do not meet men for coffee or drink dates. Five percent will hang up the phone after saying okay and goodbye. Ninety-five percent will say, "Okay, I understand," and they'll schedule a proper date with you. They might tell you that they need to think of a restaurant where the two of you would meet, and that they will call you later with a few restaurant suggestions. Sometimes they will ask you where you'd like to go; give them a few names of restaurants that you like, and let them decide.

Some men have been known to call women over a period of months to see if they have discounted themselves enough to accept a coffee date. Keep telling them the same thing: "Thank you for calling; when you are ready to spend quality time with me and invite me to sit down and eat a meal with you, I'll be happy to meet with you." There are no good reasons why you should discount yourself for a man who has issues about taking you out to dinner. You are not on sale in the bargain basement section. If they want to spend bargain basement prices, they can keep shopping for another woman.

Some men will call your first date a "meeting," and that is why they suggest coffee only, because for them it is not a date. To these men, tell them that you reserve "meetings" for business purposes only and that you are dating to find a mate, not to get a new client. Any man who does not want to pay for your dinner in order to have a date with you doesn't have enough money. Period. Men who can afford it gladly pay to have the company of a lovely woman to share time with them at a restaurant, any day of the week.

Also, keep in mind that many men have been turned down when they have invited women for dinner on a first date and learned that it is safer to just offer coffee on a first date. Many men I know are relieved when a woman says that she doesn't care for coffee dates, as these men do not like feeling like cheapskates who only offer a coffee date to a woman.

A man who is serious enough and is the protective and generous type will think it is only normal that you would value yourself and your time enough not to waste it for a man who does not want to feed you. Any man who thinks that all you want out of dating is a free meal does not understand the dynamic you are looking for and won't change to become the masculine provider you need in order to give all of you to a man.

Set up the standard for the life you want to live. If you do not set the standards, don't be upset if you do not get what you want.

If you want to accept coffee dates or drink dates, go ahead. But make sure that you do not over give of your time to a man you will only meet for a coffee or drink date. This is where many women become resentful of the men they are dating. Over giving has a way of eating at your feminine self-image. You need to manage your precious time and decide with whom you will share your delightful self. I know women who have drink dates with men, followed by dinner dates with other men. If you can make it work, good for you. I personally find it too exhausting to do on a regular basis and haven't had anything good ever come out of a drink date. I have found that these men want to have a convenient relationship in which the woman will pick up the tab equally every time they go out together.

The reason I am not in favor of coffee and drink dates has nothing to do with money; it has to do with how a man is willing to provide for you. I find it preferable for a woman to be with a man who has less money but who is generous with it and is happy to share his wealth with her than to be with a man who has more money, but who is reluctant to part with it.

Now, as in every other part of our lives, there are exceptions that we need to take into consideration. If a man invites you on a drink date because it is the only time he has before embarking on a flight to Asia for a few weeks, and he absolutely wants to meet you before he leaves, and you feel that he is genuine, by all means, go meet with him with the same enthusiasm you would any other dates. You will feel and know what will be the best thing to do. Just listen to your feelings, and act as openly and sincerely as you would on any dinner date.

EMAIL DATES

Here are a few reasons why you don't want to type your life away through emails. First, with regards to men you will meet on the Internet, know that the latest poll indicates that fifty percent of the men dating on Internet dating sites are married, and that you do not know with whom you are communicating. Email is the communication of choice for married men. They are sitting at their computers chatting with women while their wives are in the kitchen preparing dinner. You don't want to waste your time with these imposters.

You might be exchanging emails with under age young men who only want a thrill to talk sexy to a grown up woman, and this obviously could become a problem you don't need in your life. Or you could be communicating with a man in prison; not your first choice in partners. These are only a few reasons why I discourage spending your valuable time typing away. You will do much better meeting men in person; plus think of all the situations where you could meet your future husband while being out there dating. You could meet him while putting gas in your car on your way to your date. You could meet him while waiting for your date who happens to be late. I can go on with all the good things that can happen to you while being out there dating.

I suggest you not give any more information than what was on your profile in your emails. If they want to know more about you, they will take the necessary steps to get to know you. Send them a reply telling them that you would love to tell them more about yourself, but would feel more comfortable doing this in person and that they are welcome to call you to set up a date. That's all. Men who are serious will want to meet with you. Why do I suggest for you not to spend more time on emails and phone conversations and insist on meeting in person? Because unavailable men tend to carry email fantasies and you will grow tired of these dead end email communications and phone conversations with married or unavailable men. Why would you want to waste time shooting blanks through fiber optic wires? At least if you go on a dud date, you'll not only be practicing your dating skills, but you will also create the chance to meet your future husband on the way to your date! By wanting to meet men in person rather then chat online or talk on the phone, you will eliminate lots of heartaches. And what about the men to whom you sent your telephone number, but they did not call you? Be assured that it is because they are busy somewhere else.

Some men will keep emailing until you tell them that you do not want to date through emails. When you receive the first email from a man you feel is a potential suitor, send him back this response: "Hi Steve, thank you for contacting me. I find you interesting, and would love to know more about you. You can contact me at 555-123-4567. Paula." Or you can give him the chance to take the lead and asking you for your number or send you his, by sending him the following email: "Hi Steve, thank you for contacting me. I find your profile interesting and would love to know more about you. Please let me know how you would like us to get to know each other. Paula." Or again, you can write: "Thank you for your letter. You seem like a nice man. Gary, I do not like to communicate through emails as I find them too impersonal. If you are interested in calling me, I will give you my telephone number. Please let me know what you want to do. Paula." If they send you their telephone numbers, go ahead and call them for the initial call, and if you are still interested in them, give them your telephone number and let them take the lead in the future.

The only emails you have to send are in response to their inquiries in which you write, "thank you" and include your telephone number or ask them how they want to proceed in order for the two of you to meet. If they write to you again and want to have email communications with you, send them the same email until they call, or tell you how they want to proceed, or until they simply stop writing and go away.

Do not communicate by email. It is impersonal and misleading at best. You are serious about finding a husband, not a pen pal. If they keep writing to you, keep sending them the same email until they call. If they do not call or do not send you their telephone number, chances are their wives have called them to dinner!

Under no circumstances should you set up dates over the Internet by email. Never. You have to get a sense of the man you will be meeting, and you cannot get that from an email. You have many more chances to notice if a man is a schizophrenic, a sadist, or a maniac over the telephone than through an email. Your instincts will be sharper over the phone than they could ever be in writing. And trust your instincts. If you have a bad feeling about a man, even through an email, do not go further with that man. There are enough men out there that you do not need to compromise your safety for the sake of meeting your future husband. Setting dates over emails can only lead to confusion;

you have more opportunities to appeal to him in a feminine way by talking on the telephone than you would through emails. Emails are cold and impersonal—good for business, yet lousy for personal interactions.

HANG OUT DATES

I discourage hang out dates because they usually lead into bed faster than you have the chance to figure out what just happened. Unless you are in a committed relationship, please do not do hang out dates. What do you have to gain to drive to a man's place or him to yours to hang out and watch television? You have better things to do, don't you? That won't give you much of a chance to meet anybody on the way, will it? Unless a man has made it worth your while to spend time cooking at home and cuddling on the sofa by giving you the commitment you need, don't even go there. It is okay if your number one date wants to relax and do something low key. Just go have a pizza, and see a movie. Hang out dates are simply "too married." If he wants to hang out at home, he can put a ring on your finger.

Don't be shy about telling a man you do not want to do hang out dates with a man you are just dating. First, thank him for inviting you to hang out at his house. Tell him that you are certainly looking forward to being in a committed relationship where you will feel comfortable doing just that on a Saturday night, since you like quiet nights at home; however, until you are engaged, you simply feel that hanging out is too intimate. Tell him that you are way too attracted to him to be hugging on a sofa without a chaperon. He will get it. Every man will get this. If a man wants only to have sex with you, he will be running for the hills, and you won't hear from him again. If he is looking for a virtuous woman to marry, he'll be even more proud of you for "hanging" to your commitments.

If your date asks you to hang out at his place, do not tell him you have other plans; tell him the truth, and let him fix this for you. If he is too tired to jump in a pair of jeans and go for a pizza and a movie, well, maybe you'll do better to put on your cutest little black dress and go sit at a popular bar or a lounge and meet someone who is a little less tired than he is. If a man is too tired to take you out during courtship, just imagine how married life with this guy will be!

Don't feel like you would be losing something by taking care of yourself and requesting to go out on proper dates. Never be afraid to lose a man either. He should be the one making sure that you want to be with him, not the other way around.

I can assure you that you will like dating much more when you allow yourself to be courted properly by men who have the interest and the energy to be in a loving relationship with a woman.

· · ·

25

Dating Men From Out Of Town

Nothing in life is to be feared. It is only to be understood.

Mary Curie

SOME MEN WILL FLY FROM ACROSS THE COUNTRY for the chance to meet the wonderful-sounding woman you have become. Men will even fly from other countries in the hope of having the opportunity to court you. Do meet and date men from out of town in the same way you would date a man who lives in your city. Dating men from out of town is not a reason to let your guard down. Because a man comes from out of town, it does not mean that you have to be a chauffeur or a tour guide.

First of all, let's make something very clear: you don't know the men you are dealing with when you meet men on an Internet dating site, from a dating service, at the market, or even, although sometimes more reliable, through your best friend. Amber Frey met Scott Peterson, who was soon to become a convicted murderer, through her best girlfriend who thought he was nice. So keep in mind that you know nothing about these men. Even if they "look nice," it means nothing. All his neighbors thought Jeffrey Dahmer was a "real nice guy." These men may be married, sociopaths, psychopaths, rapists, or even murderers; the important point is you don't know. Read the chapter "*Safety & Security ~*

How to Stay Safe While on a Date" very carefully.

Don't be a fool. Take care of yourself. Meet men in public places where you can feel comfortable and be safe. Meeting a man in the midst of an outdoor fair is not a safe place. Any place from which a man can drag you to a deserted area is not a safe place.

With the new phenomenon of broadband phones, anyone can now get a phone number with any exchange from any state in the United States. A man might tell you that he lives in Florida, give you a telephone number with an area code in Florida, direct you to his website with an address in Florida, while in fact, he lives only a few streets from you in Chicago! How can that be? He has a broadband phone line with a Florida area code, and he made his own website with the misleading information he wants you and other women to believe. Later on, if something bad happens to you, the only information you will be able to give to the police is that he was a man from Florida and his name was... Well, of course, he used a fictitious name...

Follow these simple guidelines and you should be fine.

When a man comes to visit you from out of town, let him stay at a hotel. Do not let him stay with you at your house. Also, let him rent a car so that he can transport himself from the airport to his hotel and then meet you at the restaurant or meeting place you have both agreed on. Do not pick up a man at his hotel because he didn't rent a car or because he doesn't really know the city well enough. It is not your job to take care of him. He is a grown man and can take care of himself in your city as well as he can in his own city. Remember, you don't yet know if he lives in your own neighborhood or not.

If he asks you to pick him up at the airport, tell him that you do not feel comfortable with this and would prefer for him to make arrangements for his own transportation. Don't tell him to rent a car, and don't give him the phone numbers of the rental car companies. You are not his mother; let him make his own arrangements by himself. He might just prefer to take taxis when visiting a new city. Let him be a man.

If he asks you to chauffeur him around town on your outings, just repeat the same thing you told him previously regarding his transportation to his hotel. If he asks you why not, tell him that you do not feel comfortable having a strange man in your car, and that it is not that you do not want *him* in your car, but for security reasons, you do not give rides to any man you do not know. Period. Do not vacillate on this one. If he seems not to understand your need for security, perhaps it would be best not to invest any more of your time in such a man.

If a man comes to see you for many days, you do not have to spend all your free time with him. When he and you schedule the time you will spend together, just schedule the time you feel comfortable with. It can be very tiring to spend a lot of time with a new person you are getting to know. Do not hesitate to tell him when you would feel comfortable to meet with him. Here's an example of how you can voice your preferences:

He: "I can make a flight reservation to arrive Friday at 4:00 P.M. and leave on Sunday at 9:30 P.M. We would be able to spend the whole weekend together. Would you be okay with that?"

You: (You will thank him for his offer and tell him what you feel comfortable with.) "That sounds great. I am very much looking forward to meeting you. For right now, I would feel comfortable committing to have dinner with you on Friday and Saturday nights. If we really hit it off and we both enjoy each other's company, perhaps I will feel comfortable to commit myself to spend more time with you."

Then shut up and let him decide what he wants to do. Do not tell him his trip will be too long, that he should schedule only two days, and so on. Let him make the decision by himself.

He: "Oh, okay, I understand. Well maybe I will arrange to leave on Sunday morning then. I will think about it and call you back."

By letting him know what you feel comfortable with and

allowing him to make the decision of how long his trip will be, and by not trying to control everything, you will eliminate much stress and won't feel obligated to spend a whole weekend with a man you do not know yet. If you see that the two of you like each other, and you feel comfortable seeing him more than your scheduled time, then just be spontaneous, and see him more. You have nothing to lose by waiting to have the chance to know him a little better, and you will feel more comfortable making that type of commitment.

If a man insists that you have to spend the whole time with him or that you would have to drive him around town for him to come to meet with you, thank him and tell him that you will respect his decision, whatever it might be, but will have to decline. Do not back down on your safety. If a man cannot or refuses to understand that you need to be comfortable and feel safe, then perhaps he is not the man for you.

Do not go to a man's hotel room for a nightcap unless you plan to spend the night and have sex with him. Would you go to a man's house and sit with him in his bedroom? No! Then do not do it in a hotel. If you accept his invitation to go to his hotel room, any man will think that you are willing to have bedroom play with him. It is safe to have a nightcap in the lobby of his hotel, but not in his room. If he tells you that he brought you a gift and that it is in his room, tell him you'll wait for him in the lobby while he goes and gets it. Use good judgment, and try not to drink too much alcohol, which might make it harder for you to resist his persuasive ways; no alcohol would be better.

After you know your dates better, you will be more relaxed. But with any new man you meet, please keep your eyes and ears open, and protect yourself.

Keep saying "No" to what you do not feel comfortable with, and say "Yes" to what feels good to you. As long as you take care of yourself and put yourself first, you will not mind dating men from out of town.

I promise, on my honor, to date men from out of town the same "safe" way I date men who live in my town. So help me God.

26

Accepting & Setting Up Your First Dates

*In every phenomenon the beginning
remains always the most notable moment.*

Thomas Carlyle

THE TIME HAS COME TO SET UP YOUR FIRST DATES. The best thing to do is to be organized. Get a spiral notebook in order to take notes about the men who will call or whom you will call yourself. Keep track of your dates' names, phone numbers, date and time you will meet, where you will meet, and notes about what they tell you. For example, write their places of birth, birth dates, where they live, what type of work they do, or any other pertinent information you might think is worth keeping. Also get a calendar where you will record all your dates' names and phone numbers; it will make it easier for you to juggle all your dates and keep track of all of them; having their telephone numbers beside their names will make it easier for you to call them should you have to cancel a scheduled date. Get a timer in order to contain your phone conversations to the five-minute limit. Prepare a list of a few restaurants or meeting places in your living area that you would feel comfortable to go to if the men ask you for suggestions.

Before we go on, I want to talk to you about etiquette regarding calling a potential date. Preferably, men will most of the time be the ones to initiate the first phone call. If you should be the one calling, call him before 8 PM. If he gives you his work number and you call him after business hours, just take this opportunity to leave him your phone number on his voice mail, and then the ball will be in his court. If you call him and he answers the phone, always ask if this is a good time for him to talk to you. If he says "Yes," proceed, and if he says "No," take this opportunity to give him your telephone number, and be off the hook about doing the calling.

If he asks you to call him back in ten minutes, please, if you agree to it, do so. If he says he is in his car and cannot take your number, and he asks you to call him in the morning, if you can do so, say "Okay," and call him the morning after. As soon as you will have had the first conversation with him, you don't want to be the caller/pursuer anymore, as he now has your telephone number.

Always try to be as nice as possible, even if you are extremely annoyed. Be polite; you will never gain anything by being arrogant with a man or in trying to educate him. It never works.

If you have been introduced to a man through an Internet dating service, then you will have had the chance to write back and forth through emails a few times and give him your telephone number.

When he first calls you, try sounding as happy as possible. Remember to put a big smile in your face before you answer the phone.

Here's an example of setting a first date over the telephone:

Ring, ring...

You: Hello... (smiling with a languorous sound in the back of your throat...)

He: Hi, Stella, this is Kent!

You: Ohh, Kent, how nice to finally speak with you (with a surprised pleasant tone coming through that beautiful smile of yours). How are you?

He: I am fine, thank you. How are you?

You: Oh, I am fine too.

He: Regarding our meeting, I was thinking that we could meet for coffee Thursday night...

You: Oohhh, Thursday night sounds like so much fun, but I'd rather meet when you have more time for us to spend together.

He: What do you mean?

You: Well, when you have time for a real date, you know. Dinner or lunch...

See how much more pleasant that sounds? Think "Southern Belle," and you'll reel them in like salmon in springtime.

OR...

He: "Hello, Paula, this is Roger Porter from the Internet dating service. Thank you for giving me your telephone number. How are you?"

You: "Hi, Roger. I'm fine. How are you?

He: "I am fine, thank you. Do you have the time to chat right now?"

You: "Yes, of course, I do."

He: "Along with the fact that you are very pretty, I read on your profile that you like horseback riding. Last Sunday, I went to the Dude Ranch in Santa Barbara. Have you ever been there?"

You: "No, but I have heard it is a really nice place. Certainly a place I would love to visit sometime."

There you go. You already have something in common.

He: "I am sure you would like it. The estate is very beautiful. Well, would you like to meet with me for a drink, or perhaps dinner?

You: "Yes, I would like to meet with you for dinner."

He: "What is your schedule like? How about next Friday night?

You: "Next Friday night works great for me!"

He: "Would you like to meet in your neighborhood, or do you have a preference where you would like for us to meet?"

You: "Yes, meeting in my neighborhood would be great." (Tell men you live in an adjacent neighborhood to your own in order to keep you safe. Please refer to the chapter *Safety & Security ~ How To Stay Safe While Dating.)*

He: "Are there any restaurants you would prefer to go?"

You: "Yes, there are many very nice restaurants around here. I like Grande Steak House. They serve beef, of course, and the best chicken potpies and creamed spinach. I also like…"

Give him three choices. If he asks you if you want to make the reservation, tell him you prefer that he would make it. Ask him when he will be calling you to confirm your date. Most of the time, men won't know what to say about that because, usually, women never ask them to confirm their dates. They might say "Sure, no problem, when you do want me to confirm?" They need to ask that because they really don't know when to do that. Tell him that on the day of the date around noon would be perfect. He will make a note of that and will confirm with you around noon. Always ask men to confirm your dates with you so that you do not show up to be stood up, although it can still be a good way to meet men. I have been stood up a few times and always ended up meeting someone else while waiting for my date.

You have just given your date his first assignment. Men love assignments as long as they are asked with respect, and they feel that they could say no without you becoming unraveled. As you keep on dating men, you will find that they really like to do things for women. Masculine men do. When you know a man well enough to allow him to pick you up at your home, make sure that you have a little assignment for him to do. It might be that you need to change the five gallon filtered water bottle on the water stand, or that you have a case of juice in the garage that needs to be brought up to the kitchen, or that you have a picture frame that needs to be hung, things like that. I have had men I dated tell me that although they liked me, they ultimately did not want to commit to marriage. I always thanked them for their honesty and would ask them if they would be willing to help me with some projects around the house, and in exchange, I would cook anything they wanted to eat. I would playfully (and respectfully) call them my "Cabana Boys." They all got quite a kick out of that one and most fabulous meals too! Don't hesitate to ask men to do things for you, as long as you are fun and playful about it. Men love to *do*!

Also very important: let him introduce himself first to you. From the first moment the two of you meet, let him lead and decide what type of energy he wants to give to your relationship. If he is nonchalant in his body language and does not seem to make an effort to even introduce himself to you properly and make you feel at ease, then you will know this is the type of man he is, and the type of life he can offer: a nonchalant one. If he is eager to get your attention and introduces himself first and wants to make you feel comfortable, then this is the type of man he is: a man who is eager to please. Which type do you prefer?

If you arrive at the restaurant and the man acts as if he hasn't seen you (it unfortunately happens more than you think), just stand by the hostess desk and wait for him to make the two or three steps necessary to get to you and properly introduce himself. Unless his sight is very poor, and he genuinely hasn't seen you, I have to sadly say that I have never seen a relationship in which the man was passive on the first introduction work for a feminine woman, because these men tend to be feminine and passive, and as you know, it doesn't serve a feminine woman to be with a feminine man. I always say that you only have one chance to make a good first impression. Let him show you his true colors. Just stay put and let him approach you. And do not feel bad for him just because you think the poor thing is too shy to come and greet you. Do not go introduce yourself. If you do, you will end up in a relationship where you are constantly the pursuer. And who wants that? If he turns out to be that passive type of man, let him go to a woman who doesn't know better; you do!

If your date arrives late, please do not blast him, and don't tell him "You're late, I have been waiting for you, and you have made me feel bad." It will make you sound like a nag. Either do not wait for him and leave, or be gracious when he shows up. If you are too hungry to wait for him at the front door, ask the hostess to sit you at a table, or go sit at the bar, ask for a menu, order an appetizer, or ask for some bread and butter. I suggest you eat something before going on your date so you don't become ravenous if you must wait for a table, or grow irritated if the service is slow.

Have fun with your men. Do not put pressure on yourself regarding your dates. All you have to do is show up, look good, and smell good. No need to impress your dates anymore. Think "Southern Belle." Let them be nervous and try to impress you. There is always one who is more nervous than the other, so let it be your date. You will have more fun than ever and will get more from the men you date than you ever have had in the past. Now go on, start practicing, and have fun.

. . .

Dear Fléchelle,
I met a man through a dating agency, and after speaking with him over the telephone, he asked me out for dinner for our first date. I had seen pictures of him, and he had seen pictures of me. I arrived at the restaurant right at the time we had planned to meet. He was sitting at the bar when I walked in, and I smiled at him. He looked at me and then turned his head and watched the television that was playing behind the bar. I was so taken aback by his reaction that I just sat at the bar, waiting for him to gather his courage to come to speak to me. I had been there for about five minutes when a gentleman came to talk to me. A friend of his arrived about five minutes later, and we talked for about ten minutes. They then asked me if I was waiting for a friend, and I told them that I was the date of the man sitting at the bar who was

so intently ignoring me. Not to toot my horn, but I was looking pretty good that night, and there were no men in the restaurant who had not seen me and given me approving glances, other than my date, of course. The two gentlemen invited me to have dinner with them, and I accepted since it was obvious my date was not going to even acknowledge me.

My date then went home, called the agency, told them that I had not shown up and that he was very upset. I came home to an angry message from the woman at the dating agency who had set us up. The day after, I spoke to her and told her that I had been there and that he had chosen to ignore me and so I accepted dinner with the two gentlemen who asked me. She thought that I had been horrible in treating my date so poorly and should have been more sensitive towards his feelings, as he probably had been intimidated by my looks. I was mad that she would treat me as the guilty party in this situation. I don't feel that I should have done anything differently. What do you think? Suzy

Dear Suzy,

I could not have done it better myself. The agency was entirely wrong in treating you this way. They have the right to cater to feminine men who want to be chased by women, but to chastise a woman for acting as a feminine woman is simply not right. They probably don't know any better though. I would not expect to get an apology from them. Ask the agency to reimburse your money, as they clearly are not a good match for you. Go find another agency that will honor you and your femininity.

· · ·

27

Safety & Security ~ How To Stay Safe While Dating

Diligence is the mother of good fortune.

Benjamin Disraeli

YOUR SAFETY IS OF THE UTMOST IMPORTANCE. Most men you will meet will probably be good men who are seriously looking for a woman to be in a relationship with. But until you know him better and have had the chance to investigate his intentions towards you, you have to protect yourself. Here are a few safety practices for you to adopt to ensure your safety when dating strangers.

GET AN ANONYMOUS EMAIL ADDRESS

Get a dedicated email address to use while dating, which will be completely anonymous. There are several sites that offer this service for free, such as Yahoo and Hotmail. When you sign up for your email address, choose an email address that will describe you, without using your name—you could use something like "Stunning1" or "GentleOne." Anything that feels good to you, without giving the receiver a clue about your real name. The email service will ask you for your name, address, and personal information. Do not write your real name; use a pen name instead. This could be the name you choose to date with. For example if your real name is Veronica Stewart, you might want to tell potential Internet dates who ask you that your name is Veronica Smith. This way, if you meet a weirdo, he'll have one less chance to find your whereabouts. So, when signing up for an anonymous email address, use a pseudonym, and do not give your real birth date, which is another way to find out personal information about you. If you were born on July 7, 1978, write something like July 18, 1979. Use this email address only for dating on the Internet. Do not use this address for shopping on the Internet or to belong to Internet chat boards, as your posts might appear in search listings if someone makes a search on your email address. Make sure you do not provide this email address for anything that you would want to keep private.

A woman I know was found by her high school sweetheart after having written her real name when posting her opinion on a peace oriented website, where she also used her anonymous email address. In a case like that, a man might search for your anonymous email address on the Internet and find out your real name this way. So, as you can see, one can never be too careful.

GET AN ANONYMOUS MAILING ADDRESS

Get a mailbox at a private mailbox company where you can receive mail and packages. Use this address when men ask you where they can send you flowers. A friend of mine used her mailbox address this way and gave it to a man who wanted to send her flowers. Later on, she received an angry phone call from him saying that he had shown up at the given address with flowers and realized it was not her home address. He screamed at her for making him waste his time. Can you imagine what could have happened if my friend would have given him her real home address? She would have had to deal with a deranged man at her doorstep. The last thing you want is to have to deal with a crazed man who might force himself into your house. Be careful, and stay safe.

Have your car registration paperwork sent to your mailbox

address too, so if a man tries to find out where you live by using your car's license plate number, he'll have your mailbox address instead of your home address. If you can have your driver's license addressed to your mailbox address (in certain states, as long as the Department of Motor Vehicles has your home address on file, it will write your mailbox address on your driver's license itself), then do it. Have your mailbox address printed on your checks too. Have all your mail sent to this address, and give it out whenever you are requested to provide an address.

GET AN ANONYMOUS PHONE NUMBER

Get a "smart" ring on your home phone to give to your dates. This number, which usually will ring twice on your home telephone, cannot be traced to your name or your home address (check with the phone company that provides your phone services). It is a safe way for you to let men have access to you without jeopardizing your anonymity. Moreover, in having a different ring for your dates, you will know it's a date calling, so make sure to put a smile in your face, laughter in your throat, and answer "Hello" in your happiest voice possible; men will think you are in a happy mood all the time, a real plus for many men I know! Ask your telephone company about their confidential services. They get these kinds of requests every day. Having a cellular phone can also be a safe alternative for you. Make sure the service provider understands your need for privacy, and can provide you with a service that will allow you to protect yourself.

WHEN MEETING A STRANGER FOR A FIRST DATE

Unless your date is a man whom you have known for years or was introduced to you by friends or family members who have known him *very well* for years, he is a *stranger*. If you met him at the store, on the Internet, in a coffee shop, or on the street, you know nothing about this man. Good common sense is a must to assure your safety. Here are a few tips on how to conduct yourself to minimize getting into an unfortunate situation:

Give a family member or a friend all names, phone numbers and all other pertinent information you have on your dates. This way, if something happen, they'll have something to trace you with.

Do not allow men to come and pick you up at your house. You should not tell a stranger where you live, where you work, or any personal information that might allow him to get to you or hurt you.

Meet men at public places where there are a lot of people around: places like restaurants, coffee shops, and hotel lobbies. Do not meet men on the corner of a street, on a street, or in a parking lot. It takes less than ten seconds for criminals to stop a van in front of you, get you in the van and abduct you. You might think that these things do not happen and are farfetched. One only needs to listen to the news for a few days to realize that such things happen to good people every day. The best thing to do if you are going to be dating on the Internet is to visit a few restaurants or coffee shops where you will be meeting your dates and tell the personnel at these establishments that you will be dating on the Internet and would appreciate their giving you special attention during your dates. Needless to say, you should never drink too much on a date, so tell the restaurateur that you never drink enough to become inebriated and that you can always walk out of a restaurant by yourself, so if they see one of your dates carrying you by the armpits outside the restaurant, stop that man and call the police, as he might have drugged you. You should also tell the attendants at the valet parking that you are dating on the Internet and ask them to watch out for you when you exit the restaurant. Do not park your car in a remote area or in a parking structure where you could be hit on the head and stuffed into the trunk of your car.

Arrive at your meeting place at least five minutes before the agreed time. This will give you the time to use the bathroom before sitting down with your date. Do not get up during the meal or leave your drink or meal unattended. A criminal could put drugs in either your food or drink and have his way with you later on— this situation has happened too many times for me to mention. If you are meeting at a restaurant, and your date is already sitting at the table, and there is a glass of water for you on the table, when the waiter comes to your table, give it to him, and ask for a clean glass. If your date takes offense to that, it is his problem. You do not have to do anything that feels uncomfortable for you. You can even end a date at any time if you feel you should. Finding a husband doesn't mean that you have to put your life in danger. Better to be safe than sorry.

After dinner, if he offers to take you for a drink or dancing in another part of town, and you want to go, take your own car. Tell him you would feel more comfortable driving yourself, as you do not really know him yet. If he is a gentleman, he will appreciate that you take care of yourself. If he gets angry or upset with you, and tries to make you change your mind and pressures you to let him drive you, excuse yourself, and say that you are not feeling that well after all and would rather go home. Thank him for the evening, and leave at once. You do not want to be with a man who does not cherish your feelings, especially on the first few dates—it won't get any better as time goes by.

If after the evening, upon waiting with you for the valet to bring your car, your date tells you that he is parked a few streets down and ask you for a ride, say "No." You do not want to risk finding yourself in a precarious position with a man you do not know in the confinement of your car. If he asks you why, just tell him that you do not feel comfortable having someone ride in your car whom you do not really know yet. If he is a good man, he will revel in your taking good care of yourself. If he gives you a hard time, you'll even be happier you did not allow yourself to be pushed by this man into a possible unfortunate outcome.

What if he insists on picking me up at my house on our first date?

Tell him: "Thank you so much for offering to pick me up;

however, I would feel more comfortable meeting you at the restaurant." If he insists, just say: "Thank you again, but when I feel comfortable, I'll let you know." Then shut your mouth. Let him speak next and tell you what he thinks about it. If he bullies you, tell him that you'd rather not meet after all and hang up the phone. Chances are he will just say "Okay." A good man will appreciate you for taking good care of yourself.

What if he insists on making the destination of our first date a surprise and needs to either pick me up or send a limousine to pick me up?

Thank him for his exciting offer; however, since you do not know him yet, you would feel more comfortable meeting at a restaurant in your neighborhood. Assure him that when you know him better, you will be very appreciative of his initiating such fun filled evenings.

What if, upon hearing that I do not feel comfortable being picked up at my home, he says he can pick me up at the location of my choice, such as a restaurant or a bookstore?

One of the reasons you do not want to be picked up is that you want to be in control of your physical safety. Tell him that you will feel more comfortable when you know him better. Repeat that when you will know him better, you have a feeling that you will greatly appreciate his initiatives.

He won't take no for an answer. What should I do?

He obviously does not hear you and is not taking care of your feelings. Tell him that you would rather not meet after all. If a man doesn't listen to you and makes you feel uncomfortable over the telephone, listen to your feelings. It rarely will feel better in person. You are required to date anyone who has a heartbeat unless you feel that there is something morally, ethically, or legally wrong with a man. Your safety is first and foremost, and your feelings are a gauge to allow you to take care of yourself.

Do not have sexual conversations with men on the telephone

when you schedule your first meeting or on a first date, for that matter. If a man wants to talk about sex on the phone before your first date, chances are he is fishing to see if he will be able to get into your pants after dinner. There is something wrong with having a sexually loaded conversation with someone you have never met. Not because it is wrong to talk about sex, but if you are looking for a long-term relationship with a husband who will cherish you, you have an interest in sounding like a virtuous woman, not some casual fling. When a man is thinking of you as a sex object and is talking to you on that sexual level, he is not seeing you as wife material. Of course, men see women as sexual playmates, which is great, but in a cherishing and respectful way. If a man talks to you about sex on the telephone, just tell him that you are not interested in sharing this type of information with a stranger and that you are looking for a long-term relationship with a gentleman, not just a casual affair.

Here are a few pointers to adhere to when dating strangers:

> Do not allow strangers in your house when alone.

> Do not drink much alcohol when on a date unless you are with someone you know really well and feel safe with. Not drinking any alcohol at all would even be better.

> Do not have sex talk with a man you do not intend to have sex with. Talking about whips, leather outfits, and spanking risks bringing strange characters into your life. Honestly, that type of talk would scare most men I know.

> Always act ladylike if you want a man to respond to you in a gentlemanly manner.

> Do not expose too much of your body on the few first dates. Your dating uniform acts as a barrier to protect you from too much touching. You can have sex appeal and still look sexy without looking

provocative. You want to look approachable on your first dates, not necessarily touchable.

Meet men in public places, preferably in restaurants whose staff know you are there on blind dates and can keep an eye out for you.

Be accountable for your words and actions.

Please, once again, do not allow strangers in your house. In doing so, you are putting your life in danger.

Most of all, listen to your gut feelings. In his book *The Gift of Fear*, Gavin De Becker teaches people how to listen to the survival signals that protect us from violence. "People don't just 'snap' and become violent," says De Becker. "There is a process as observable and often as predictable, as water coming to a boil."

If you have a bad feeling about a man, simply do not meet with him. There are enough good men to date without putting your life at risk.

•   •   •

Dear Fléchelle,

I just posted my profile on an Internet dating service, and although I am really excited about all the possibilities available, I am somewhat scared. Can you tell me about some safety practices I might learn about in order to insure a safe and pleasant dating experience? Marianne

Dear Marianne,

I am happy to help you with this. First, I would suggest that you get an unidentifiable telephone number. Call your phone company to learn about its options. Get a caller ID. Listen to what men are telling you, and be discerning in deciding whom you are going to meet. Second, listen to your gut feelings; lots of red flags occur in the first phone conversation. Third, meet with your dates only in public places such as coffee shops and restaurants. Insist on meeting where there is a valet parking service. You do not want to be alone with a stranger, even if it is just to walk to your car. A criminal could hit you on the head and drive away with you in the trunk of your car to a deserted area. Fourth, do not share personal information such as your real name, address, and company name where you work. Go to the rest room before you are seated at the table, so you will not have to leave your food or drinks alone with a stranger for even a minute. Do not drink any beverages that were served before you arrived. Men have drugged women this way more times than I care to mention. Lastly, use good common sense. Not all men are dangerous; however, you are taking a risk in meeting strangers whom you know nothing about. Keep your eyes and ears open. Good luck in finding a loving man to cherish and protect you!

· · ·

28

Dealing With Feelings Of Rejection While Dating

Sadness flies away on the wings of time.

Jean de La Fontaine

LADIES, WHEN A MAN YOU ARE DATING (but not having sex with) says: "I want for us to just be friends," he wants to break up with you without hurting your feelings. Either that, or it might be that he is not certain he is ready to give you (or anybody) the commitment at this time that you need. Either way, you have to respect his wishes. Because you multiple date until you are in a committed relationship, you can stay open and say yes to his request of friendship. Will you? I know it hurts to be only friends with a man to whom you are attracted and about whom you had high hopes, but by keeping him around, you will have the chance to show him that you are the lady he is looking for. He might go out with others, have sex with others, but friendship is what real relationships are built upon, and he might very well come back and become serious about you.

If you have had sex with a man and he wants to break up and "stay friends," I am afraid that it is an almost impossible task. Dr. Allen says that ex-lovers can be friends, but only after they are lovers with new people. I believe that to be the truth, but by then,

211

who wants to be friends with an ex-lover anyway? So better let this one man go completely, unless he comes back with a much better offer than "just being friends."

When a man you are dating takes the time to call you and tell you that he will not be seeing you anymore, thank him for his kindness in letting you know. Most men will just stop calling and will consider you informed that they will not be seeing you anymore. You might take this opportunity to tell him how you feel about him, and if you had hoped for a future together, let him know. You can tell a man that you are disappointed because you had hoped he would have chosen you. You never know what will transpire in the future, and he might very well reconsider you again as a life partner for him in the future.

Do not call a man who hasn't called you. Chances are he has decided you were not a match for him and simply doesn't have the courage to call you to let you know. It takes a very courageous man to call a woman and tell her he won't be seeing her again, especially if they have been somewhat intimate.

Do not call a man to ask him why he isn't calling you anymore. What do you want him to say? "I don't like the way you laugh"? "I don't like the way you smell"? Give yourself a break and just move on to the next man who will be interested in you. Do not take it personally when a man breaks up with you. It rarely has anything to do with you.

I know it is hard not to think about the loss of men we care about, and this is why I suggest that women not allow themselves feelings of love towards men who have not committed themselves to them with a formal engagement. It is simply not safe for a woman to feel "in love" and share emotional intimacy with a man who is just a date. It is already hard enough to break up with a fiancé or a husband without going to this level of trauma with someone who is just a date. We allow ourselves feelings of love towards a man only after he has given us the commitment we need and want in order to move forward in a relationship. Easier said than done, but if you can manage to multiple date and keep your heart protected from the "smooth talkers" or those great men

who would make such wonderful husbands if "they would only commit to you," you will be at a much better advantage in the trenches of the dating world.

If you have acted in a way you know to be wrong and are the cause of a man leaving you, apologize to him and let it be. If he cannot get over whatever it is you did, there is nothing you can do about it. You can only learn from your mistakes, move on, and do the best you can with the next man. Don't be too hard on yourself. We all make mistakes and know that as Friedrich Nietzsche said: "That which does not kill us makes us stronger."

The best way to apologize to a man and let him know you are sorry is to leave him a message on his voice mail. Call him at home or at work when you know he is not there and leave him a message that would sound something like this: "Hi, Paul, this is Cynthia. I am calling you to apologize for (whatever it is you did), and I just wanted for you to know that I am very sorry for having (disrespected you, belittled you, unappreciated you, or whatever it is you did), and I hope that you will forgive me because I care a lot about you. If you decide not to see me anymore, I will respect your decision, but I wanted to make sure you knew how I truly feel about you. Please accept my apologies. Bye." It is okay to show your vulnerability here. Even if you cry while leaving him this message, it is okay.

The reason I think it is better to leave a message for a man instead of writing him is so he can hear in your voice your sincere intentions and your true feelings. And leaving him a message instead of talking to him directly is better because you don't want to call him while he is busy doing something else or at a time when he would not be ready to hear you out. With a message he will have the opportunity to listen to it on his own time and more than once.

If he calls you back and seems a little dry but still wants to see you, don't panic over this; it is just that you will need to regain his confidence in you, and in time you will. If he doesn't call you back, let it go. You did the best you could.

Give yourself lots of self-care, go to the spa and have a

massage. Have hot bubble baths, pamper yourself with new cozy pajamas, get yourself a good book and a pound of chocolate truffles. And keep on dating. Chin up, yours is on his way.

.　　.　　.

Dear Fléchelle,
My fiancé left me just before last Christmas. I learned it from his friends who told me they were sorry to hear that we were no longer with each other. I asked them what they meant, and they said that Les told them we had parted as friends. I never confronted him on that and never heard from him again. Now it has been five months and I need closure. Please help. Julie

Dear Julie,
Write yourself a letter "from him" to "you"—something that would say: "Dear Julie, I am writing to you to apologize for the pain I have caused you. I am a coward and my cowardice did not allow me to be a real man for you. You are such a wonderful and special woman; you deserve a real man in your life. Please forgive me. Les." You are much better off without him. Good luck.

29

Positive Mantras &
Wise Sayings

Is there anyone so wise as to learn by
the experience of others?

Voltaire

MANY YEARS AGO, A FRIEND OF MINE TOLD ME: "Never go to bed with a man who has more problems than you do." This is one of the best pieces of advice I have ever gotten.

Here are a few mantras and wise sayings you can add to your repertoire. Some will fit, some won't. I just hope you can have fun with these and perhaps even gain some insights on every day life. Enjoy.

Live your life as if today were your last day.

Be kind to others.

Try something new every day.

Never let rotten apples touch good ones.

Things happen for a good reason.

Smiling will give your face muscles a workout.

Don't let jealous or envious people run your life.

Stand up for your rights.

Know when to say "Yes". Know when to say "No".

Gracefully accept compliments. Eagerly give compliments.

Feel twenty again, everyday.

Make the best of what you've got.

Happiness is the fulfillment of our expectations.

I do my best, and my best is good enough.

Smile with your eyes, laugh with your heart.

A healthy soul lives in a healthy body.

Be thankful for all you have.

Laugh at least three minutes every day.

Take a walk in the rain.

Don't take yourself too seriously.

Laugh at yourself any chance you get.

Keeping an open heart is a great way to attract beautiful people in our lives.

30

Questions & Answers

*One's mind, once stretched by a new idea,
never regains its original dimension.*

Oliver Wendell Holmes

HERE IS A COMPILED SELECTION OF QUESTIONS I have received and their answers.

Q: What if he tells me that he will go away if I don't kiss him?

A: Thank him for his honesty, and tell him that you'll miss him terribly.

Q: What do I say if he tells me that he would never be able to get engaged to a woman unless he has kissed her passionately?

A: Thank him for his honesty, and tell him that you will respect his decision.

Q: What if a man tells me he could never get engaged to me if I do not give him sex?

A: Thank him for his honesty. Tell him that you respect his decision and that you'll miss him terribly.

Q: Won't a man think that I am not interested in him if I don't kiss him?

A: Not if you are receptive to him and treat him with respect. A man who is really interested in you will find out what he has to do in order to make you his.

Q: What if a man asks me to go away for a weekend and I want to, but don't know him enough to share a room with him?

A: Tell him that you would love to join him, however you would need your own room. If he says you can have your own room at your own expense, decline. If he says that he'll be happy to provide you with comfortable accommodations, go and have a good time.

Q: What if he tells his friends that we are intimate, although we are not?

A: It is his right to choose to introduce you to his friends the way he wants to. If you do not like him to misrepresent you in this way, you can either ask him to fix it, or leave him.

Q: What if his friends tell him to be wary of me?

A: If his friends lack respect for him enough to tell him what to do, and he takes their advice, that's his problem. You can either accept it or leave him.

Q: What if his mother tells him he needs to try me out before getting engaged?

A: If his mother lacks respect for him enough to tell him what to do, and he takes it, that's his problem. Masculine men seek respect from their mothers the same way they expect respect from all women in their lives. If he is not masculine enough for you, leave him.

Q: What if my girlfriend tells me that I am crazy to be on the "No Kissing Plan"?

A: How much do you pay your girlfriends for their advice? Nothing? This is what their advice should be worth to you. Tell them you appreciate their concerns, but that you are a competent woman and can take care of yourself.

Q: But "The Rules" say not to accept a date for a Saturday night later than on Wednesday night?

A: You are not following "The Rules." You are out there having a good time with good men, not punishing them.

Q: What if a man tells me he won't continue to see me unless I stop dating others?

A: Men are by nature territorial, so when they are interested in a woman they do not want any other men to have her. Ask him if he is proposing to you by any chance. If he is not proposing, and still wants you to give him exclusivity without a commitment, and threatens he will no longer see you if you do not give in to his wishes, tell him that you'll miss him terribly.

Q: What if a man tells me that it is too big an investment to buy a ring for me before having had sex?

A: Tell him that you understand, say that it would be too big an investment for you to give yourself to him without a ring and a formal commitment.

Q: What if I lose him because I do not want to give him sex?

A: You cannot lose someone you never had.

Q: What if a man tells me that he cannot fall in love with me unless we have sex first?

A: Run for your life! No, just kidding. Thank him for being so honest with you, and tell him that one of the reasons you do not want to rush into bed with a man and need a serious commitment is that you need to feel safe in knowing that he loves you before you can make love with him. If he cannot fall in love with you without sex, and you cannot make love with a man who is not in love with you, then you have an irreconcilable difference, that's all.

Q: What if a man tells me that it is impossible for any men to fall in love without having sex first?

A: First, this man doesn't know what he is talking about, but you won't tell him that, right? Men fall in love all the time with women they have no chance in the world of ever getting near. Simply tell him that you respect his thoughts on the subject.

Q: What if a man calls me past my bedtime to chat or set up a date?

A: Let your answering device take the call for you. Return his call the day after, and tell him that you are sorry you missed his call as you were already asleep. He should get the drift.

Q: I find it difficult not to think of the men I am dating and fantasizing about a future life with them, especially the ones I like the most. What can I do not to think about them so much?

A: You are not dating enough men simultaneously. They are only dates (and practice) until they commit to a relationship with you. You cannot take men seriously until THEY are serious enough to put a ring on your finger first!

Q: But I don't want to lead men on if I know I wouldn't want to marry them.

A: You are not leading them on. You are giving them the opportunity to become better men for having known you and having had the chance to go out with a respectful and appreciative feminine lady. You need to practice your dating skills so that when a good one shows up, you'll know what to do. If you meet men whom you have no interest in at all after three dates, you might want to stop seeing them, but only if you have quite a few others in the wings. Otherwise, let them lead and decide if you are interested enough in them or not. Besides, you never know if one of these men might grow on you; perhaps one of them would end up treating you well enough for you to decide to let him take care of you.

Q: What if I meet a man, and he says he is serious, and I really like him. Should I keep dating others?

A: They all are dates until one of them gives you a ring and offers you the commitment you need. In the meantime, date, date, date. Do not stop dating because one man is great for right now. What if he turns out to be a frog in three months? You might lose the opportunity to meet your future husband while you are playing with Mr. Wrong. And if he turns out to be Mr. Right, that will be great. In the meantime, go out with this little darling and have fun, but keep on multiple dating until you are off the market with a ring and a formal engagement.

Q: I want so much to let this man I date kiss me. Should I?

A: Of course, if you want to let him kiss you, do so and enjoy... There is just more of a risk to fall in the short-lived relationship trap if you lose your brain to oxytocin, that's all. To help you keep your pants on, just keep thinking about the feelings a woman has after giving free sex to a man who says, while pulling his pants up, "I hope we can still be friends..." You have the right to say yes to whatever you want. Or no to whatever you do not want.

Q: Should I call a man to thank him for a great evening?

A: Do not call or send email to a man to thank him for a date. It is the masculine thing to do. He is the one who has to call you, on his schedule, to thank you for *your* time.

Q: Should I ask men to make plans with me in advance? I don't like it when my number one calls me and I already have other plans.

A: No, you do not ask men to change the way they court you. When your number one calls, cancel your other plans, and go out with him. You can also try to train him by telling him you have other plans, and let him figure out to call you sooner in the future. However, just keep in mind that he might just be very busy. Play it by ear, and if you feel the man is genuine, just give him a break and go out with him. What do you have to lose?

Q: A man I date always takes me out during the weekdays, always asks me what I am doing on the weekend, but never asks me out on Saturday night. What does that mean?

A: About his asking you if you had plans for the weekend, it is just because he is fishing to see if you are doing something with someone else. Just know that if he is not with you on Saturday night, it is because he is with someone else. Saturday night is "date night." Next time he asks you what you are doing on the weekend, here's your answer: "Nothing." Then if he is only fishing, you'll know, as he will not ask you out. And if he is serious about you, and does not have obligations somewhere else, he'll invite you out.

Q: What if I cancel a date with a man in order to go out with someone, and he shows up at the same restaurant and sees me with another date?

A: Just smile at him if you see him looking at you, and go back to your business with your date. If he comes to you and asks you what you are doing, just introduce both men, and tell him that you are busy but will be happy to speak to him when he next calls you, and wish him a good night. Chances are he is not going to go so far as asking you what you are up to. He will certainly get that you are on a date. You are a single woman going on about your life, and you do not owe anything to any man with whom you have no commitments. And who could be upset at you for taking care of yourself?

Q: What if men ask me to call them if I feel like it? I don't like to be the pursuer.

A: Thank them for the offer, but say that you would feel more comfortable waiting for their phone calls. And leave it at that.

Q: One of my dates is inviting me to have dinner at his house. I am very attracted to him and feel almost as if I am playing with fire. Do you have any good advice for me not to fall into his very inviting arms?

A: If you think you are playing with fire, it's probably because you are. Do not go to a man's house and let him cook dinner for you unless there are other people there. Meet men in public places, or if you must have dinner at his home, again have it with friends. And when the friends leave, leave too. It is way too intimate and you will probably be putting yourself in a situation that will be hard to get out of, especially if you are attracted to him. A man who invites you to have dinner at his place (alone) will be (in most cases) thinking that sex is also on the menu (unless you have been seeing each other for a while, and have both already discussed your boundaries, and are both willing to wait until engagement before having sex); I would wonder about him if he wouldn't think that sex is on the menu. If you are just dating a man without having had any serious talks with him, just be extra careful, and know that "dinner at his place" is one of the oldest tricks in any man's book.

Q: There is a man at work I am attracted to and he seems to like me too. I feel that he would like to approach me and talk to me. What should I do to let him know that he is welcome to approach me?

A: Be professional. When you see him, if it is appropriate, you can signal him by looking into his eyes for five long seconds while smiling. If and when he approaches you for a one-on-one conversation, be sweet and feminine. When around other people, be as you always are at work. If he asks you to go on a date with him, go and be sweet and feminine. The way he will "personally" know you is the way he will think of you.

Q: Can I ask a man out for a date?

A: No. That would be chasing. If he's not interested in you enough, or he's not man enough to ask you out, you should let it go, and go out with the men who ask you.

Q: I asked a man I date if he thinks we have a future together, and he told me he doesn't know if we are enough of a good match. Do you think there is a chance?

A: Anything else but a "yes" is a "no". And stop asking men questions about a future together, or where your relationship is going. Instead, let men pursue you and try to track *you* down.

Q: What if a man asks me to go to his house after a date?

A: Say: "Thanks, how sweet, but I'm not comfortable with that right now." If he asks when you will feel comfortable, give him "The Talk."

Q: A man I really love has stopped calling me. I just cannot get over it and have been unable to go out. Is there anything I can do to feel better?

A: Yes, you are supposed to go out and have a good time. Remember, you are not supposed to attach yourself to a man who has not attached himself to you first. The way you are acting shows that you love him more than you love yourself and obviously more than he loves you. You have to discipline your thoughts. If you want him to come back, stop putting so much energy into him—he can feel it by the way.

Q: I want to have sex with one of my dates. I am not so much attracted to him but I like him as I find him fun to be around. I think there are some exceptions, and we should take a different look at all the different situations. What do you think?

A: Sure, if you want to take that risk, go ahead, but you might wake up in three years from now and be in a relationship as an unhappy free wife instead of a happy married one.

Q: Should I sometimes pay on dates?

A: I do not recommend it as I feel it shifts the energy between a man and a woman. Let the men pay, and give them back by giving them a portion of a home cooked dinner you've made, or giving them a music compact disc, or a book they mentioned being interested in. Give back to them, but always in a smaller amount than they gave. You don't want to top them with gifts. Let them be the providers.

Q: I contracted a sexually transmitted disease years ago. I have not had any recurring effects from it, but I know that I am a carrier. How can I tell a man I date about this?

A: Preferably, you would wait for him to ask you about sexually transmitted diseases, or wait to be engaged, but most certainly before having sex you would tell a man about your sexually transmitted disease(s). If you do not want to wait for a commitment from him first, then I suggest you have a "Have you had a sexually transmitted disease?" talk with a man, but only after you have had "The Talk" about commitment, ring, and so on. For example, if you tell a man about your needs of being engaged with a ring, and he still hangs around, then already the relationship has moved to another level, right? If he is still courting you and has gotten to know you better, and you feel comfortable enough that he is not going to run for the hills, then during a date, just bring the subject up casually. For example, you might ask him if he ever has contracted a sexually transmitted disease, the same casual way you would ask him if he ever went to the circus when he was young. I think the best way (when he gives you his answer about if he ever contracted a sexually transmitted disease or not) is to just say: "Oh! Have you? (Or "Oh! You never?) And then say, "Well I have had..." or "I have..." while keeping it light. You can also tell him that you do not mind talking about it if he has any question that comes to mind, now or later. You can also ask your doctor or internist how you can discuss this very sensitive subject with a potential future mate.

I would not bring this up with a man you're just dating. It is way too much information for him, and unless he sticks around, he is not going to find out all about the precious you!

Q: Do you think that men know that when we cuddle, kiss, and have sex with them, we get bonded?

A: Yes, men know that if they could only get into the pants of a woman, she'll be his.

Q: What does that mean if a man tells me that unless I have sex with him, he'll go somewhere else?

A: That means that a man is trying to intimidate you into having sex with him. He has poor communication skills, cares more about his needs than your feelings, and tries to bully you into jumping in the sack with him. A masculine man will not try to cowardly coerce you into having sex with him; he will try to win your heart. He certainly won't threaten you to not be there for you unless you have sex with him. I suggest you let him go have sex with others. If he cares more about you than he does himself, then perhaps he will grow up and step up to the plate and learn how to cherish your feelings above taking care of his physical needs. Don't hold your breath though, and date others.

Q: What should I do when men insist I have dessert after a meal? I like to keep a good figure and do not want to eat those extra calories.

A: Accept the dessert, eat a few bites (eat three less bites of your meal if you must), have the dessert wrapped to take home and throw it in the trash upon arriving home if you do not have anybody to give it to. It will be great practice for you to be saying yes to what men offer you. Men complain all the time that women don't want to eat. The same thing goes if he gives you a gift you do not like; just say "Thank you" and put it away.

In Closing

Come to the edge," he said.
They said, "We are afraid."
Come to the edge," he said.
They came.
He pushed them...
And they flew.

Guillaume Apollinaire

I hope I have helped you make better decisions about whom you will choose to give your kisses to and choose as a future husband. Hopefully, you are now ready and willing to go out there, date, and meet the best husband for you.

My next book is about helping you build solid foundations with the man from whom you will have accepted a ring, an engagement, and a promise of a future married life together. This book will cover the period from engagement to marriage. There is much to learn about one another during that period, along with numerous conscious negotiations to be made in order to form a strong and enduring long term relationship. The art of negotiation during the engagement period is a learned tool and a valuable asset to possess for the survival of a young flourishing relationship. You will learn how to make your relationship's environment safe—a safe environment is a must in order to communicate the truth between partners. You will learn to avoid the pitfalls that can lead a good and promising relationship to a regrettable end before it even had a chance to begin.

I am very much looking forward to presenting you with this upcoming book as I know it will greatly help you in your next chapter towards successfully reaching your dreams of marriage and creating your family. You can look for its availability on my website at www.nokissing.com.

I am looking forward to hearing from you, and you are welcome to write to me at flechelle@nokissing.com. Please let me know if my book has helped you improve your perception about dating, or even perhaps expanded your understanding of men. I would love to know if it has helped you to be found by a good man whom you have chosen, and with whom you finally feel happy. You can post your success story on my website at www.nokissing.com. You will also find more information about dating at www.nokissing.com.

You can contact me for one-on-one consultations or for me to be a speaker at your company or event. I am happy to speak to small and large groups alike. You can reach me at (877) 2NO-KISSING or (877) 266-5477. You can also write to me at:

Cheval Publishing, Inc.
Attn.: Fléchelle Morin
P.O. Box 664
Pacific Palisades, CA 90272

Until then, I wish you all a most beautiful day!

Bibliography

Allen, Dr. Patricia (Pat). *Conversational Rape.* 1987.

Allen, Dr. Patricia (Pat) and Sandra Harmon.
Getting To "I Do". New York: Avon Books, Inc. 1995.
Staying Married And Loving It. New York: Avon Books, Inc. 1998.

de Becker, Gavin. *The Gift of Fear.* New York: Little, Brown and Company. 1997.

Behrendt, Greg and Liz Tuccillo. *He's Just Not That Into You: The No-Excuse Truth To Understanding Guys.* New York: Simon Spotlight Entertainment. 2004.

Pease, Allan and Barbara. *Why Men Don't Listen and Women Can't Read Maps.* New York: Broadway Books. 2000.

Per permission to excerpt from *The Art Of Living*, by Wilferd A. Peterson, published by Galahad Books, permission granted by Heacock Literary Agency, Inc.

· · ·

Index

. . .

Order Form

Email: orders@chevalpublishing.com

Web: www.chevalpublishing.com

Telephone: Call (877) 243-8251 toll free.

Fax: Please call us to get our fax number at (877) 243-8251.

By mail: Cheval Publishing, Inc.
P.O. Box 664-001
Pacific Palisades, CA 90272, USA

☐ **Please send me the book** *Kissing Or No Kissing: Whom Will You Save Your Kisses For?* I am guaranteed that I can return the book for a full refund for any reason.

Sales Tax: Please add 8.25% for books shipped to California.

Shipping by air:
U.S.: $4.00 US
International: $10.00 US

You can pay by check or credit card:
☐ **Visa** ☐ **MasterCard**

Card number: _____

Name on card: _____ **Exp. Date:** _____

.   .   .